LOW

Italian Arias of the Baroque and Classical Eras

John Glenn Paton, Editor

ABOUT THIS EDITION

Alfred has made every effort to make this book not only attractive but more useful and long-lasting as well. Usually, large books do not lie flat or stay open on the music rack. In addition, the pages (which are glued together) tend to break away from the spine after repeated use.

In this edition, pages are sewn together in multiples of 16. This special process allows the book to stay open for ease in playing and prevents pages from falling out. We hope this unique binding will give you added pleasure and additional use.

Cover art: by Giovanni Paolo Pannini. Oil on canvas. The Louvre, Paris / The Granger Collection, New York. The cover depicts a festive performance of *La contesa de' numi (The Contest of the Gods)* by Leonardo Vinci, text by Pietro Metastasio, at a private theater in Rome in 1729. The work is a *serenata,* or serenade, a secular work that resembles an opera in every musical respect, but is not staged. The elaborate set depicted in the painting probably was stationary and did not change during the work. The chief patron was a cardinal from France; the occasion celebrated the birth of a daughter to the French royal family.

Copyright © 1994 Alfred Music
All rights reserved. Produced in USA.

Table of Contents

Preface

This collection contains arias that are favorites on the concert programs of great singers and in voice studios around the world, and also contains many arias that are unfamiliar to modern music lovers. A preceding volume, *26 Italian Songs and Arias*, demonstrated the value of restoring the most authentic possible version of even the most familiar arias; this volume continues that restorative process.

Nine arias published here have never appeared in a modern anthology before; at least one of them, the aria by Antonia Bembo, has never been published anywhere. Others have been published before in many different editions, but for this volume they have been completely revised on the basis of early manuscripts or first printings.

In the late 1800s editors and publishers sought to reach a wide audience by "modernizing" the music of the 1600s and 1700s. In this process, editors:

• altered harmonies that seemed rough or dissonant to them.

• added words to break up long vocal runs, which were out of fashion at that time.

• altered rhythms to make them less dance-like.

• added tempo markings that are too slow, and expression marks that overly romanticize the style.

• added accompaniments in a late-Romantic pianistic style.

Over a century ago a Roman musician, Alessandro Parisotti, was working on a compilation of 100 songs entitled *Arie antiche* (Milan: Ricordi, Volume I, 1885; Volume II, 1890; Volume III, 1900). G. Schirmer, Inc., reprinted the first two volumes in 1895. The early printings of these volumes contained biographical notes about composers and photographic facsimiles of historical sources; current printings, while retaining copyright notices that lapsed long ago, omit most of those desirable features.

Preeminent among the vocal anthologies of its time, *Arie antiche* established a core repertoire that is still sung by voice students and concert artists around the world. While Parisotti's work on behalf of "ancient arias" deserves respect, he was one of those editors who freely "modernized" music of centuries past, according to the fashion of his own time. He also admittedly borrowed from the work of other editors. Fourteen songs in this volume were included in Parisotti's collection, as indicated in the source notes that precede each song. Three of those fourteen songs were borrowed by Parisotti with slight alterations from *Les Gloires de l'Italie*, edited by François Auguste Gevaert (Paris: private subscription, 1868, later by Heugel). Three more songs came from *Arien und Gesänge älterer Tonmeister,* edited by Carl Banck (Leipzig: F. Kistner, 1880). There was no international copyright at the time; Parisotti borrowed legally. (The source notes refer to Parisotti, Gevaert, and Banck by name only, without further reference to the titles of their books.)

Modern editors no longer try to "improve" the music of past centuries. Our goal now is to present the music in the most honest form possible. We believe that the best composers of earlier times still have something beautiful to give us, and we have a duty to respect their music without willfully changing it.

If you have known these arias in other editions, you will find surprises in this one. Many errors have been corrected. Wrong notes, wrong words and wrong composers' names have been set right whenever possible.

On the page preceding each aria, the singer will find vital information for an expressive and stylistic performance. The Italian poem is printed in boldface. Italian pronunciations are shown, using the International Phonetic Alphabet with certain modifications that were pioneered by the late Berton Coffin for the specific needs of singers. (A pronunciation key is found inside the back cover.) Each individual Italian word is translated literally into English. A hyphen is used where the meaning of one Italian word requires more than one English word: for instance, "M'ami?" means "Do-you-love-me?" (Because of grammatical differences between Italian and English, these translations do not always make readable sense.)

The "Poetic Idea," as summarized by the editor, is intentionally terse — it is provided merely as a safeguard against misunderstandings. If the aria comes from an opera, the character is named and the dramatic situation is explained.

"Background" is the factual story that lies behind the music: who wrote the aria, where it was written, and why it was outstanding in its time. I recommend that you use a good music dictionary to learn more about the lives of the composers than could be told here.

"Source" lists what materials were used to prepare this edition and how it differs from the versions that have been available until now.

The music pages present one more English translation, this time into idiomatic English. These translations may be used as program notes for recitals.

The vocal line of each aria has been reproduced accurately from an early manuscript or a first edition. Vocal ornaments and musical variations are often suggested in smaller notation that is clearly distinguished from what the composer wrote. In the Italian texts, phonetic symbols for open e's and o's are printed in stressed syllables so that the student can learn the correct vowel from the beginning.

Similarly, the bass line, known as continuo, is shown clearly and accurately. Most of the original figured-bass symbols in the continuo part have been included, except for some that are obvious. For instance, when the voice and continuo are a sixth apart, no figure six is printed under the bass note. Most of the time keyboard players were expected to harmonize the continuo part without help from figures.

Musicians of the 1600s and 1700s did not look far into the future. Expecting to be present whenever their music was performed, they wrote down a bare minimum of instructions for the performers. Tempo, dynamic or style markings that are printed in gray are my suggestions, not those of the composer.

The Roots of Baroque Style

The arias in this book are arranged in chronological order of the composers, so that by hearing them in sequence one gets a feeling for the history of Italian music in the Baroque (1600-1750) and Classical (1750-1830) periods. Now and then you may want to look at a map of Italy and pictures of the cities where famous composers lived so that you have a sense of them as real people who loved singing and music just as you do. (See the map of Geographical Origins on page 160.)

Baroque is a term borrowed from art history. Painters, sculptors and architects of the Baroque era broke with the strict geometrical forms of the Renaissance and strove to create an overall balance between parts that are not symmetrical. They used rich ornamentation and created surprising contrasts in order to awaken a viewer's emotions.

We can easily identify these same characteristics in the music of the era, beginning with the musical experiments of Ottavio Rinuccini, Jacopo Peri and Giulio Caccini in Florence. These and other cultivated persons in the group called Camerata speculated about classical Greek drama and how ancient Greek actors had sung their lines. Desirous of hearing such a performance, they created a new style of music that contrasted radically with the music of the preceding period, the Renaissance.

Renaissance vocal music was either sung in churches, where the Latin texts were not understood by most people, or in homes, where sociable people sang part-songs for their own enjoyment. In either case, singers did not sing with individualized, dramatic expression because they took on subordinate roles in groups.

Solo singing as we know it began when Peri and others composed music in which a soloist sang dramatically, accompanied by instruments playing chords in the background. It became possible to sing whole plays on stage, resulting in the first operas. This experiment was the basis of the Baroque style.

An essential part of the new style was the practice of writing bass-notes so that they indicated what chords should be played by the accompanying instruments. A typical small performing ensemble was a singer, a cello, and a harpsichord or lute. The instruments played from a single line of music, called a *basso continuo* because it is always present. The cello sustained the bass-notes, which often had melodic interest that formed a counterpoint to the voice. The harpsichord added appropriate chords. How the chords were added was up to the player. Since few modern pianists know how to play from a basso continuo, modern editions must provide written-out piano parts.

The Evolution of Classical and Romantic Styles

The gradual transition to Classical style took place in the mid-1700s as composers wrote out accompaniments more completely and composed more often for a full orchestra of strings and sometimes wind instruments. The subject matter of operas changed, as servants and working people became operatic characters (think of Rossini's *The Barber of Seville* and Mozart's *The Marriage of Figaro).*

Vocal styles did not change greatly; great singers were still international stars, and singers were still expected to master the art of vocal ornamentation. An excellent source of information is an exercise book that appeared at the end of the Classical period, Vaccai's *Practical Method of Italian Singing*, edited by John Glenn Paton (New York: G. Schirmer, 1974). The ornaments that Vaccai illustrated are valid for all composers in the Italian tradition throughout the Classical era.

In the Romantic era, composers exerted more control over performers and refused to allow singers to alter or ornament their music. As music was written out in more and more detail, it became customary to sing only the notes that were written. On the other hand, performers were expected to "interpret" the music with frequent variations in dynamics and tempo. In a highly Romantic style of performance, every phrase may contain some crescendo or diminuendo, accelerando or ritardando. The paradoxical result is that in Romantic style, the performer is true to the notes of the piece, but gives them a personal twist.

This view of Romantic performance style explains why editors who published older music were inclined to add expression markings that altered the character of the music. Some such markings are helpful, but others convey a false impression of the music.

Tirſi Viene in ſcena ſonando la preſente Zinfonia con vn Triflauto, e canta la ſeguente ſtanza; ſalutando Orfeo di poi s'accompagna con gli altri del Coro, e con tale ſtrumento fu ſonata.

Nel pur ardor della piu bella ſtella Aurea facella di bel foc'accēdi

An excerpt showing the first twelve measures of *"Nel pur ardor,"* published in 1600. The staff lines are not perfectly straight because they are made of many pieces of movable type, a separate piece for each musical symbol.

All three instruments play from the soprano clef (middle C on the lowest line). As a help for sight-reading, there is a mark at the end of each staff, indicating the line or space of the first note on the next line.

When the voice enters it is in tenor clef (middle C on the fourth line), and the bass part is in F clef. The key is G Major, but there is no key signature. The bass note below the word *"bella"* has a sharp sign which indicates a major harmony for the chord-playing instruments; their part is not written out and must be improvised.

Good Style in Italian Singing

Baroque and Classical composers gave few instructions about musical performance; they did not foresee that future musicians would be interested. Even tempo, dynamics and style are usually left to our imaginations. We have great freedom, therefore, and great responsibility when we perform early music.

Keep in mind that expression of the words was Caccini's first priority and the motivation behind the Baroque movement. Even if your listeners do not understand Italian, they expect you to know what the words mean and to sing every word clearly. Know what each single word means, and then put yourself into the frame of mind of the character whom you are portraying. Practice speaking the words aloud with a clear, well-supported voice before you sing them. Vowels in Italian are much more important than consonants; only double consonants and rolled r's are emphasized.

Beautiful tone is expected at all times, and later Baroque composers wrote long legato runs to display singers' beautiful voices. Naturally, accurate intonation and consistent vocal quality depend on developing a secure breath technique.

While it is inherently dramatic, the Italian singing that we are studying is also a courtly art, one of graciousness and good manners. The texts are invariably about aspects of love, including joy, doubt, jealousy, and a thousand other variations, but never extending to vulgarity or violence.

The singer always appeals to the sympathy of genteel listeners, who will be offended if the singer is too self-indulgent. Erratic tempos, extreme ritardandos, facial grimaces, and uncontrolled gesticulation may be regarded as musical bad manners. Dynamic extremes, loud or soft, are hardly ever desirable.

When choosing a tempo, consider how many songs even today are written in dance-rhythms. For instance, several arias in this book are minuets, and they sound well when performed with an even, danceable tempo. Metronomes were invented around 1800, so metronome markings in early music are merely editors' opinions.

Throughout the Baroque and Classical eras, singers were considered the most important musicians; they were better paid than composers and more in demand in foreign countries. Singers were also highly trained musicians, who could read and learn music quickly and add ornaments tastefully. The best singers could improvise ornaments, so that no two performances were identical.

This edition includes suggestions for melodic ornamentation printed in cue-sized notes, but these are models only. Feel free to sing ornaments or not, as you prefer. After gaining some experience with this style, you may prefer to invent your own ornaments.

The best ornaments do three things at once:

- they make the music more expressive; for instance, a trill might symbolize a tremor of excitement in the voice;
- they clarify the music; for instance, by calling the listener's attention to an important cadence;
- they display the singer's voice; for instance, by demonstrating flexibility and wide range.

An important rule: an ornament must always sound as if it is easy for you. If it sounds uncertain or laborious, leave it out. For this reason alone, it is important to know which notes are original and which are ornaments, and this edition always makes that distinction clear.

A final word about pitch: if the range of a song is uncomfortable for you, feel free to transpose it to a higher or lower key. Music was often transposed in the 1600s and 1700s. Pitches were lower before 1800 than they are today. For instance, Scarlatti's C was almost the same as the pitch we call B today. It is always more important to make beautiful tones than to sing some specific high or low pitch.

Good Style in Accompanying

Much of what has been said about vocal style applies to Baroque and Classical instrumental music, which is also both dramatic and courtly. It is of basic importance that the pianist, as well as the singer, must understand what the text of the song says. In addition, certain technical things need to be said, especially to pianists who have little experience with early music.

Practically all early instruments were softer and lighter in tone than modern pianos. Even a full string orchestra probably made less sound than a modern grand piano. Furthermore, any music composed before about 1770 was intended for a harpsichord, which has no sustaining pedal. This music will sound best if it is played clearly and lightly.

Most of the keyboard accompaniments given here are my realizations of figured or (mostly) unfigured bass parts. They approximate the style in which experienced players improvised. When noteheads of two differ-

A page showing measures 42-48 of *"Teco, sì,"* and part of the following recitative. Most opera scores in the 1700s were copied by hand on paper that is wider than it is high. This page, shown slightly reduced, is a typical example.

The first two systems have three staves: the violin part in G clef, the voice in soprano clef, and the continuo in F clef. The continuo will be played by cello, bass, and harpsichord, and perhaps a lute as well. The aria ends with the instruction *D.C. al Segno*; the modern equivalent is *D.S.* The recitative is sung by another character in the opera, whose part is notated in alto clef. Usually, the character's name would be given, but it is omitted here.

ent sizes are seen, the larger ones are notes written for additional instruments or for an orchestra, and the smaller notes were added by the editor to supply notes that were left out of the chords. In either case the performer should feel free to alter the accompaniments to suit the needs of the singer and the resonant quality of the piano or other instrument played.

Throughout this book the bass part written by the composer is shown clearly: the original bass notes are the lowest that are printed in full-sized notes. The bass part was played by a cello or string bass, or both. Because a string bass sounds an octave lower than written, it is often appropriate to double the bass notes an octave lower if you think it will give better support to the singer. To decide this you should consider the maturity of the voice, the room where you are playing, and the characteristics of the piano in order to maintain lightness.

Rolled chords have been suggested, especially in songs that might have been accompanied by a lute or guitar. You may choose to break other chords in slow tempos, to add notes or revoice chords, and to ornament the keyboard part to your liking.

Many songs begin without any instrumental introduction. You can easily give the singer the correct pitch by playing a tonic arpeggio that ends on the singer's starting tone.

The recordings of aria accompaniments that supplement this edition are an attractive feature for the singer who does not have easy access to an accompanist. Available on cassette and compact disc, they are meant to be used for practice and rehearsal.

Acknowledgments

Thanks are expressed to the libraries mentioned in the source notes and to many others in the U.S. and abroad, to their helpful staff members, and to the governments that support them.

Enza Ferrari of Vittorio Veneto, Italy, an expert coach of Italian operatic music, advised me on the correct pronunciation of the diphthongs that are formed between Italian words in context. Greta Damrau of New York City and Dr. Roger Scanlan of Chicago assisted me on specific points of research. Parts of this book are based on research done in 1975 on a grant from the University of Colorado.

This book recalls to mind happy days when I worked side by side with my wife, Joan Thompson, sharing the excitement of discoveries in libraries in Paris, Berlin, and other cities in Europe and the U.S. Joan's contributions to my work increase with every book, and this one is clearer and more artistic than it would have been without her suggestions about both words and music.

That this research sees the light of day is owing to Morton Manus, President of Alfred Publishing Co., and a man of vision and integrity. Among the unfailingly helpful professionals at Alfred, Linda Lusk has had special responsibility for the innumerable details involved in musical editing.

John Glenn Paton, Los Angeles

Nel pur ardor

from *"Euridice"* (1600)
[euɾiditʃe]

Jacopo Peri
[jakopo pɛɾi]
(Rome, 1561 – Florence, 1633)

nel puɾ ardoɾ delːla pju bɛlːla stelːla
1 Nel pur ardor della più bella stella
In-the pure heat of-the most beautiful star,

auɾea fatʃɛlːla di bɛl fɔkatːʃɛndi
2 Aurea facella di bel foc'accendi
golden torch of beautiful fire-kindle

e kwi diʃːʃɛndi su lːauɾate pjume
3 E qui discendi su l'aurate piume,
and here descend on the-golden plumes,

dʒokondo nume e di tʃelɛste fjamːma
4 Giocondo nume, e di celeste fiamma
happy god, and with celestial flame

lanime infjamːma.
5 L'anime infiamma.
the-souls enflame.

ljɛto imenɛo dalta doltʃɛtːsa un nembo
6 Lieto Imeneo, d'alta dolcezza un nembo
Happy Hymen, of-sublime sweetness a rain

trabokːka in grɛmbo a fortunati amanti
7 Trabocca in grembo a fortunati amanti
flood into bosom of the-fortunate lovers

e tra bɛi kanti di soavi amori
8 E tra bei canti di soavi amori
and among beautiful songs of sweet loves

zveʎːʎa nei kɔri una doltʃe auɾa un rizo
9 Sveglia nei cori una dolce aura, un riso
awaken in-the hearts a sweet breeze, a smile

di paɾadizo
10 Di paradiso.
of paradise.

Poetic idea

"May our dear friends be happy on their wedding day!" The singer is a shepherd named Tirsi, who is honoring Orpheus on the day of his marriage to Euridice. Orpheus (in Italian, Orfeo) is the most famous singer in ancient Greek myths.

Shortly after this song the shocking news arrives that Euridice has died suddenly of a snakebite. Orpheus must go to the Underworld to reclaim his beloved bride.

Rinuccini was a member of the *Camerata*, the artistic experimenters who invented opera. *Euridice* is regarded as the earliest surviving opera.

Background

The Grand Dukes of Tuscany came from the family called Medici [mɛditʃi], famous for their lavish support of artists. When Maria de' Medici married Henri IV, King of France, the occasion called for the most novel and expensive forms of entertainment that could be imagined (even though the bridegroom did not go to Florence for the festivities). One splendid event was the performance of Peri's opera before an invited audience in the Pitti Palace.

Peri, an employee of the Medici court for many years, sang the role of Orpheus in his own opera.

Sources

(1) *Le Musiche sopra l'Euridice*, score of the opera (Florence: Marescotti, 1600; reproduced in a facsimile edition: Rome: Reale Accademia d'Italia, 1934). For voice (tenor clef) and continuo. Original key: G major (no signature).
(2) Libretto (Florence: no publisher, 1600), copy at Yale University.

Meter signature: 3 (most measures contain six half notes). Key signature of the aria: C (most measures contain four half notes). The first meter signature conveys a three-to-one ratio between two tempos: three half notes in the introduction are equal to one half note in the aria. This edition uses modern time signatures and original note values.

The score contains an instruction: "Tirsi comes onstage playing the present introduction on a *triflauto* [triple flute?] and sings the following stanza. Greeting Orfeo further, he accompanies himself with others of the chorus..."

The singer probably held a panpipe, and the music was played by recorders behind the scene. This edition uses an *8va* marking for the recorder parts because they play an octave higher than written. The continuo accompaniment is realized in normal notes, not *8va.*

In the original score music is printed only for the first stanza, while the second is printed separately in poetic form. Apparently the latter was sung by several members of the chorus. This edition offers both stanzas in full, with suggested ornaments for the second.

The libretto, which contains no hints about staging, spells out words which are contracted in the score: line 1, *puro ardor*; line 2, *foco accendi.*

Dr. Howard Mayer Brown has published a modern edition of the opera (Madison: A-R Editions, 1981). The aria has been anthologized by Luigi Dallapiccola (New York: International, 1961) and by Anthony Lewis (London: Associated Boards of the Royal Schools of Music, 1983).

Nel pur ardor

Ottavio Rinuccini

Jacopo Peri
Realization by John Glenn Paton

Idiomatic translation: With the pure fire of the most beautiful star,

ⓐ This is the original notation, but in practice the quarter rest and two eighth notes may be played as if they were a half rest and two half notes in the new meter and tempo.

light a golden torch of beautiful flames and come down on golden wings, smiling god, and light our souls with celestial flames.

ⓑ Sing each vowel as a quarter note.

Happy god of marriage, pour a flood of sublime sweetness into the hearts of the happy lovers and, during beautiful songs

of gentle love, awaken in their hearts a sweet breath, a smile of paradise.

Vezzosette e care pupilette

from *Libro primo di villanelle* (1616)
[libro primo di vilːlanɛlːle]

Andrea Falconieri
[andrɛa falkonjɛri]
(Naples, ca. 1585 – Naples, 1656)

vetːsozetːte kare
1 Vezzosette e care
Charming and dear

pupilːletːte ardɛnti
2 Pupillette ardenti,
little-eyes ardent,

ke va fatːto avare
3 Chi v'ha fatto avare
who you-has made stingy

dei bɛi rai lutʃɛnti
4 Dei bei rai lucenti?
of-the beautiful rays shining?

sio rimiro i vɔstri zgwardi
5 S'io rimiro i vostri sguardi,
If-I gaze-at the your glances,

skɔrgo sol fulmini e dardi
6 Scorgo sol fulmini e dardi,
I-discern only lightnings and darts,

ne veder sɔ pju kwel rizo
7 Né veder so più quel riso
nor to-see I-know more that smile

ke rendea si vago il vizo
8 Che rendea si vago il viso.
that rendered so pretty the face.

non pju zdeɲːɲozetːte
9 Non più, sdegnosette,
Not more, disdainful-ones,

rimirar vi vɔʎːʎo
10 Rimirar vi voglio,
to-see you I-want

ne pːpju superbetːte
11 Né più, superbette,
nor anymore, dear-proud-ones,

sofːfrir tanto orgoʎːʎo
12 Soffrir tanto orgoglio.
to-suffer such haughtiness.

ke veder sio non vofːfezi
13 Che veder, s'io non v'offesi,
Because to-see, if-I not you-offended,

vɔstri rai di zdeɲːɲo atːʃezi
14 Vostri rai di sdegno accesi,
your glances with disdain lit,

pupiletːte ɛ indʒusto dwɔlo
15 Pupillette, è ingiusto duolo.
dear-eyes, is unfair suffering.

o ridete o prɛndo il vɔlo
16 O ridete, o prendo il volo.
Either smile or I-take the flight.

Poetic idea
"What makes you look so angrily at me, when I love you and have done nothing to hurt you?"

Falconieri was probably the poet of this song, as well as the composer and first performer. If this is true, he resembled John Dowland and other lutenists of Elizabethan England, who wrote, composed, sang and accompanied their own songs.

Background
In the early 1600s many books of songs with simple accompaniments were published commercially for the enjoyment of both professional and amateur musicians. Many such books used a system of chord symbols devised for a five-stringed "Spanish guitar" tuned A2, D3, G3, B3 and E4. Some books provided a chart that showed where to place the fingers on the strings for each symbol. The letters used as chord symbols were not the names of the chords; for instance, G stood for an F major chord and K stood for a B♭ minor chord.

The *villanella* is a light, popular song of a type that originated in Naples. The name comes from the Italian words for "rustic" and "peasant." Because a *villanella* was thought of as being simple, it was allowed to have a certain harmonic crudeness that was not allowed in more refined music. For example, chords were often used in stepwise parallel motion, resulting in the parallel fifths that were forbidden in polyphonic music. Such chord movement appears in measures 16-20, where the bass line descends scale-wise and every bass note is the root of a chord.

Source
Libro primo di villanelle (Rome: Robletti, 1616), Biblioteca musicale governativa del Conservatorio di Musica "S. Cecilia," Rome, page 4. For voice (soprano clef) and continuo, with chord symbols. Original key: F major.

Line 16 above originally read: *O ridete, o io prendo volo*. The non-essential pronoun *io* has been dropped because there is not enough time to pronounce four vowels clearly.

Parisotti published this aria with an introduction which he composed. He avoided the harmonic roughness discussed above by inserting other chords to break the scale-wise pattern.

Vezzosette e care pupillette

Andrea Falconieri
Realization by John Glenn Paton

Allegretto, ♩ = 100–110

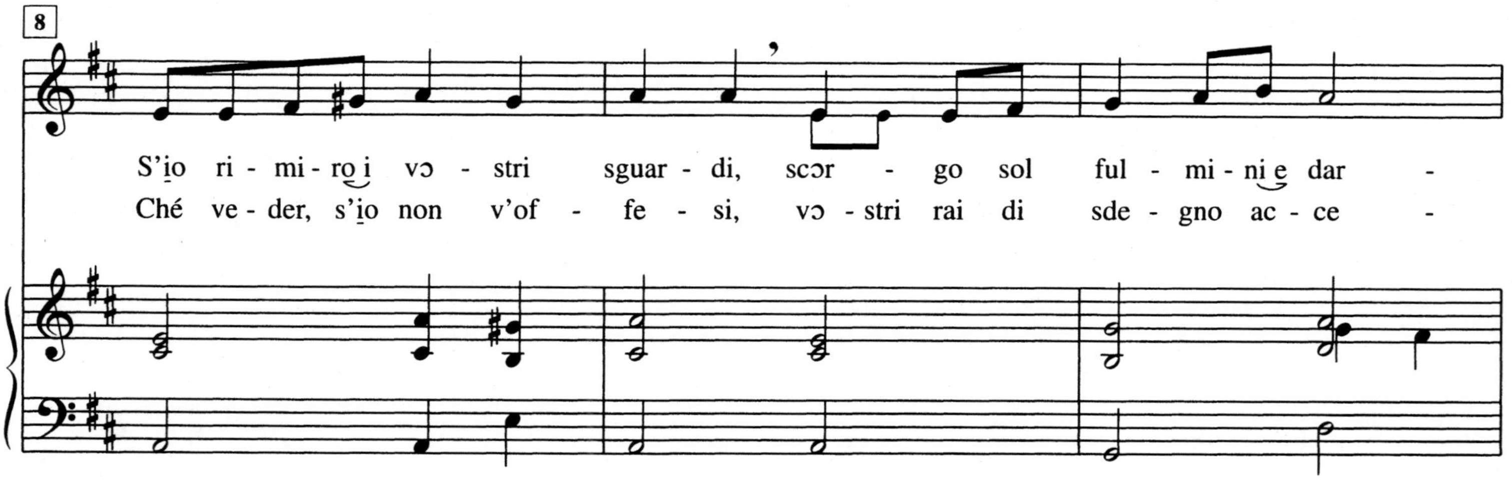

1. Vez - zo - set - te e ca - re pu - pi - let - te ar - dɛn - ti, chi v'ha fat - to a - va - re dei bɛi rai lu - cɛn - ti, chi v'ha fat - to a - va - re dei bɛi rai lu - cɛn - ti?
2. Non più sde - gno - set - te, ri - mi - rar vi vɔ - glio, né più, su - per - bet - te, sof - frir tan - to or - go - glio, né più, su - per - bet - te, sof - frir tan - to or - go - glio.

4

8

S'io ri - mi - ro i vɔ - stri sguar - di, scɔr - go sol ful - mi - ni e dar -
Ché ve - der, s'io non v'of - fe - si, vɔ - stri rai di sde - gno ac - ce -

Idiomatic translation:

1.) Lovely and dear little eyes so ardent, who made you so miserly with your bright glances?
If I gaze at your glances, I see lightnings and darts; I can no longer see the smile that made your face so pretty.

2.) I don't want to see you looking disdainful, nor do I want to suffer from such haughtiness. Because if I have not offended you, to see your glances on fire with disdain, dear eyes, is an unjust pain. Either smile or I will go my way.

ⓐ If an interlude between stanzas is desired, repeat measures 26–27, piano part.

The stanzas given above are the first and third of Falconieri's original poem. These are the words of the original second stanza:

Chi v'ha fatto oscure,	Who has made you dark,
pupilette belle,	you dear, beautiful eyes,
Che serene e pure	that when bright and pure
rassembrami stelle?	seemed to me like stars?
Chi m'ha tolto i dolci rai?	Who has taken the sweet eyes from me?
Dillo, Amor, se tu lo sai!	Say it, Cupid, if you know!
Dillo, e sia quel che si fia	Say it, whether it is caused by
O disprezzo o gelosia.	scorn or jealousy.
Vezzosette, etc.	*(Refrain)*

Che t'ho fatt'io

from *Il primo libro delle musiche* (1618)
[il primo libro delːle muzike]

Francesca Caccini
[frantʃeska katːʃini]
(Florence, 1587 – Florence, 1640)

ke to fatːtio
1 Che t'ho fatt'io,
What to-you-have done-I

ke tanto brami
2 Che tanto brami
that so-much you-desire

la mɔrte mia perke io non tami
3 La morte mia perché io non t'ami?
the death mine because I not you-love?

non sai kio vivo sol del tuo splendore
4 Non sai ch'io vivo sol del tuo splendore?
Not know-you that-I live only from your splendor?

ai duro kɔre oimɛ pjɛgal dezio
5 Ahi, duro core! Ohimè, piega'l desio!
Ah, hard heart! Alas, bend-to-the desire!

6 Che t'ho fatt'io?

se sprɛtːsi amore
7 Se sprezzi amore,
If you-scorn love,

iŋgrato seno
8 Ingrato seno,
ungrateful bosom,

dʒa non voler kio vɛŋga meno
9 Già non voler ch'io venga meno.
indeed do-not will that-I become less (die).

gradiʃːʃi almen kio tami e kwel tormento
10 Gradisci almen ch'io t'ami, e quel tormento
May-it-please at-least that-I you-love, and that torment

kio per te sɛnto ai dispjetato kɔre
11 Ch'io per te sento, ahi dispietato core,
that for you I-feel, ah cruel heart,

12 Se sprezzi amore.

Poetic idea
"Why are you so cruel to me, when I love no one but you?"

Like Falconieri, the composer of the *"Vezzosette e care,"* Caccini was probably poet, composer and performer, all in one versatile person.

Background
Francesca Caccini's father was Giulio Caccini, the composer of *"Amarilli, mia bella"* and a member of the Camerata.

Caccini made her professional debut as a singer just after her 13th birthday, during the royal wedding celebration which included Peri's opera *Euridice*. In 1607 she became a salaried employee of the Medici court in Florence. Besides being a brilliant vocal performer, she composed a successful opera, *The Liberation of Ruggiero from Alcina's Island,* which was performed in Florence and Warsaw, thus becoming the first Italian opera ever performed outside of Italy.

This aria begins as if it were part of a conversation that is already underway: the first melody tone is on the second scale degree, harmonized with an inverted dominant chord.

The third measure presents an enigma: The harmonic interval between voice and continuo is an unprepared ninth, and the next interval is a seventh. If Caccini were a more conventional composer, one would assume that there is a misprint here and invent a more consonant bass part. Remembering the daring harmonies of *"Lasciatemi morire"* by her contemporary, Monteverdi, I offer here a harmonization that keeps the dissonances.

Source
Il primo libro delle musiche, copy at Bibliothèque Nationale, Paris, Rés. F.24. For voice (soprano clef) and continuo. Original key: G minor, signature of one flat. The meter signatures are 3 (most measures contain six half notes) and C, but the proportions found in *"Nel puro ardor"* do not work here. A practical solution is to sing half notes twice as fast in the first tempo as in the second.

Only the first stanza of text is printed with the music; the others are printed in verse form following the music. *"Se sprezzi..."* is the last of four stanzas.

In this edition the first stanza is given as Caccini wrote it, and the fourth is ornamented in a style appropriate for the period. The remaining stanzas are printed after the music. I have added an interlude, measures 21-22, that is not in the original.

Caccini's book has been published in facsimile in the series *Italian Secular Song*, Vol. I (Hamden, CT: Garland, 1986). Unfortunately, this song is illegible in the facsimile because photographic copy does not distinguish between the printing on the page and other printing that has bled through the paper from the reverse side. In using the original book, one sees the difference easily.

This aria has never before appeared in an anthology.

Che t'ho fatt'io

Francesca Caccini
Realization by John Glenn Paton

ⓐ Sing the three vowels as a quarter and two eighth notes.

Idiomatic translation: 1) What have I done to you, that you so much desire my death for not loving you? Do you not know that I live only for your beauty?

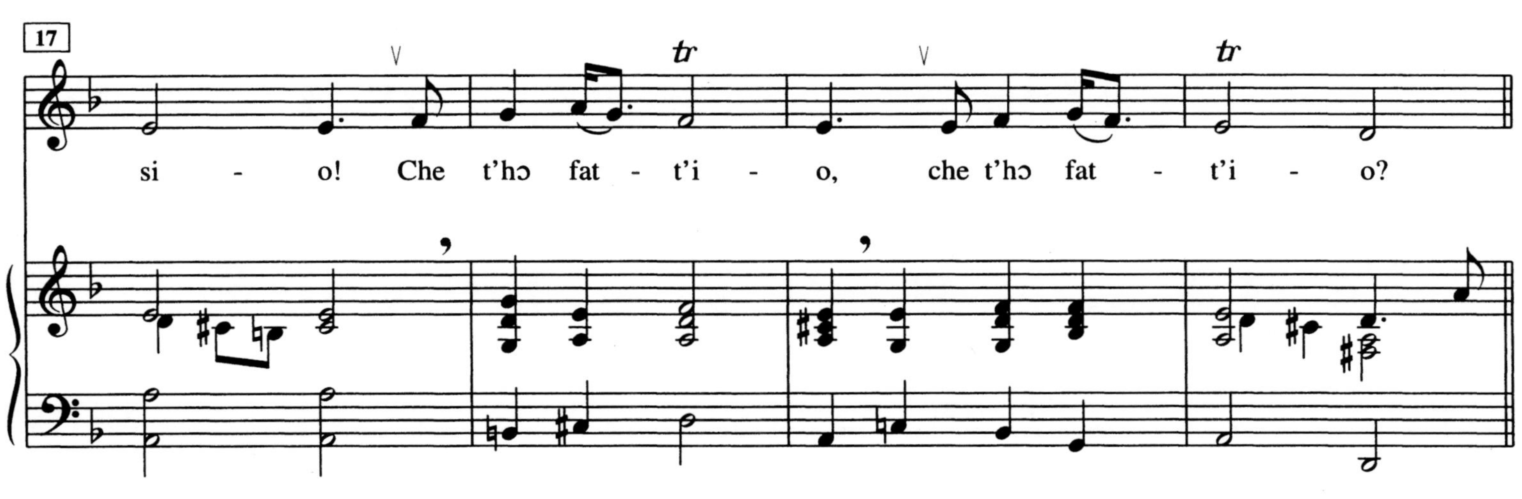

Ah, hard heart! Alas, yield to my desire! What have I done to you? If you scorn love,

ungrateful heart, at least do not wish for me to die. May you at least be pleased at my loving you and at the torment

that I go through for you. Ah, cruel heart! If you scorn love!

These are the second and third stanzas of Caccini's poem:

Che vanto avrai
Ch'io mi consumi
Al chiaro Sol de' tuoi bei lumi?
Deh, volgi al mio dolor pietoso il guardo,
Ch'io moro et ardo. Ahi, se morir mi fai,
Che vanto avrai?

D'un alma altera,
Ria crudeltate,
Pregio non sia d'alta beltate,
Ma di fedele amor, di pura fede
Empia mercede, ahi cor di crudo seno,
D'un alma altera.

Piangete

(Undated)

Giacomo Carissimi
[dʒakomo karisːsimi]
(Marini, 1605 – Rome, 1674)

pjandʒete oimɛ pjandʒete
1 **Piangete, ohimè piangete,**
Weep, alas, weep,

anime inːamorate
2 **Anime innamorate,**
souls in-love,

e sokːkorso e pjetate
3 **E soccorso e pietate,**
and comfort and pity,

sospirando pjandʒɛndo altrui kjedete
4 **Sospirando, piangendo, altrui chiedete.**
sighing, weeping, of-others ask!

kwando sadira belta serena
5 **Quando s'adira beltà serena,**
When herself-angers beauty enchanting,

ki non sospira indarno spɛra
6 **Chi non sospira indarno spera.**
whoever not sighs, in-vain hopes.

ki non pjandʒe damar non si dia vanto
7 **Chi non piange, d'amar non si dia vanto.**
Whoever not weeps, of-loving not himself may-give boast.

ɛ fɔko amor e lo sostjɛne il pjanto
8 **E foco amor, e lo sostiene il pianto.**
Is fire love, and it sustains the weeping.

laŋgwite oimɛ laŋgwite
9 **Languite, ohimè languite,**
Languish, alas, languish,

o segwatʃi damore
10 **O seguaci d'Amore!**
o followers of-Love!

il tormento il dolore
11 **Il tormento, il dolore**
The torment, the pain,

ne sospiri ne pjanti altrui ridete
12 **Né sospiri, né pianti altrui ridete.**
Nor sighs, nor tears of-others laugh.

se dira ɛ pjɛno un bɛl sembjante
13 **Se d'ira è pieno un bel sembiante,**
If of-anger is full a beautiful face,

ki non vjɛn meno ɛ falso amante
14 **Chi non vien meno è falso amante.**
Whoever not comes less is false lover.

ki non pjandʒe damar non si dia vanto
15 **Chi non piange, d'amar non si dia vanto.**
Whoever not weeps, of-loving not himself may-give boast.

konoʃːʃe amor i swɔi segwatʃi al pjanto
16 **Conosce Amor i suoi seguaci al pianto.**
Knows Love the his followers by-the weeping.

Poetic idea
"You lovers must suffer without expecting sympathy or relief. That is the nature of love."

Background
Carissimi is best remembered for the dramatic impact of his oratorios, which are musical settings of stories from the Bible, using all of the emotional resources known to opera in his time.

Carissimi also composed about 150 pieces of a new type called the *cantata.* The word simply means "sung" and it describes music that is sung, *musica cantata*, rather than music that is played, *musica sonata.* Later the word cantata took on the meaning of a choral piece to be sung in church, but in Carissimi's time almost all cantatas were secular.

Early cantatas for solo voice and continuo were written in a great variety of forms from simple one-part songs to extended pieces in many movements, taking ten minutes or more to sing. Experimentation was boundless in musical respects, but there was only one supreme subject matter, romantic love, in all of its forms from flirtation to high passion to raging jealousy.

Source
Manuscript copy of this aria only, Civico Museo Bibliografico Musicale, Bologna, Ms. X.235. For voice (soprano clef) and continuo. Original key: G minor (signature of one flat).

Repeat signs indicate that measures 1-21 may be sung twice and also that measures 22-41 may be sung twice. These optional repetitions might be highly ornamented.

The first stanza is complete and satisfying in itself. The manuscript contains a second stanza of text; it is given here on a separate line to show: (1) some rhythmic adaptations needed to fit the words to the music; and (2) possibilities for ornamenting a vocal line as singers might have done in the early 1600s. Both the rhythms and the ornamentations are only my suggestions; they do not come from the composer. Many of the ornaments can be used appropriately in the first stanza, if one chooses to sing only one.

Although da capo arias were not being written in Carissimi's time, Parisotti transformed this piece into one by repeating the first section after the second section.

Piangete

Poet unknown

Giacomo Carissimi
Realization by John Glenn Paton

ⓐ The version on this staff comes from the editor, not from the composer.
The ornaments are intended only as examples of ornaments used in Carissimi's period.

Idiomatic translation:

1) Weep, alas, weep, you souls that are in love! And with sighs and tears beg other people to help and pity you!
2) Languish, alas, languish, O disciples of Love; do not laugh at the torment, the pain, nor the sighs nor the tears of others.

5
na - mo - ra - te, e soc - cor - so e pie -
gua - ci d'A - mo - re! Il tor - men - to, il do -
4 3
7
ta - te, so - spi - ran - do, pian - gɛn - do, al - trui chie - de -
lo - re, né so - spi - ri, né pian - ti al - trui ri - de -
6♯
10
- te, e soc - cor - so e pie -
- te. Il tor - men - to, il do -
4 3

12
ta - te, so - spi - ran - do, pian - gɛn - do, al - trui chie - de -
lo - re, né so - spi - ri, né pian - ti al - trui ri - de -
15
- te. Pian - ge - te, ohi - mɛ̀, ohi -
- te. Lan - gui - te, ohi - mɛ̀, ohi -
17
mɛ̀ pian - ge - te! Pian -
mɛ̀ lan - gui - te! Lan -

1) When a tempting beauty becomes angry, anyone who is not sighing must be hoping in vain!
2) If a beautiful face is filled with anger anyone who does not weaken is not really a lover.

1) Anyone who is not weeping cannot boast of being in love. Love is a fire that is kept alive with tears.
2) Anyone who does not weep, should not boast of loving. Love knows his disciples by their tears.

36
lo so - stiɛ - ne il pian - to, il
suɔi se - gua - ci al pian - to, al
38
pian - - -
pian - - -
40
- - - to.
- - - to.

Dimmi amor

(Undated)

Arcangelo Lori
[arkandʒelo lɔri]
(Birth unknown – Rome, 1679)

dimːmi amor dimːmi ke fa
1 Dimmi, amor, dimmi che fa
Tell-me, love, tell-me what is-doing

la mia kara liberta
2 La mia cara libertà?
the my dear freedom?

dakːke andɔ kome sai tu
3 Dacché andò, come sai tu,
Since it-went, as know you,

alːlegarsi ad un bɛl krine
4 A legarsi ad un bel crine,
to bind-itself to a beautiful hair,

kwesto kɔr pjɛn di ruine
5 Questo cor, pien di ruine,
this heart, full of ruins,

non a pɔi rivista pju
6 Non ha poi rivista più.
not has then seen-(it)-again more.

un pensjɛro il kɔr mandɔ
7 Un pensiero il cor mandò
A thought the heart sent

a trovarla in sue katene
8 A trovarla in sue catene,
to find-it in its chains,

ma per kreʃːʃer le mie pene
9 Ma per crescer le mie pene
but to increase the my pains

il pensjɛr mai non tornɔ
10 Il pensier mai non tornò.
the thought ever not returned.

kwel pensjɛr kesːsi parti
11 Quel pensier che sì partì
That thought that thus departed

restɔ forse pridʒonjɛro
12 Restò forse prigioniero,
stayed perhaps prisoner,

kinːnamora oɲːɲi pensjɛro
13 Ch'innamora ogni pensiero
because-charms every thought

la belta ke mi feri
14 La beltà che mi ferì.
the beauty that me wounded.

Poetic idea
"I have lost my freedom. Where did it go? My beloved holds it captive."

Background
Lori was a Roman musician who was so closely identified with his instrument, the lute, that he was referred to as Arcangelo *del Leuto* [del lɛuto], "of-the lute." Documents of the church of San Luigi dei Francesi show that he played the organ there as early as 1633 and that he played the lute for festive church occasions as late as 1667, evidence of a long career.

Like the preceding piece, *"Piangete,"* this is a solo cantata in one movement. The subject is again love, and the musical form is experimental and unique: One expects the initial melody to return as a refrain, but it returns in an altered form.

Source
A manuscript collection entitled *Cantate di Rossi e Savioni*, Bibliothèque Royale Albert Ier., Brussels, Ms. II 3947, F2422.

For voice (soprano clef) and continuo. Original key: G major with no signature. Meter signature: 3.

The collection contains 35 solo cantatas by Luigi Rossi, Mario Savioni, and some other Roman composers; *"Dimmi, amor"* is the only one by "Arcangelo del Leuto." The *F* in the book's double catalog number indicates that this book once belonged to the Belgian music historian, Fétis, who composed *"Se i miei sospiri."*

"Dimmi, amor" was first published by Gevaert, who did not know the composer's correct name. It is one of altogether nine songs that Parisotti borrowed, with slight alterations, for his anthology.

Dimmi, amor

Poet unknown

Arcangelo Lori
Realization by John Glenn Paton

Allegretto, ♩ = 108–116
Dim - mi, a - mor, dim - mi che fa la mia ca - ra li - ber -
5 6
3

7
tà?
1. Dac-ché an - dò, co - me sai tu, a le - gar - si ad
2. Un pen - siɛ - ro il cɔr man - dò a tro - var - la in
7 6
4
2

13
un bɛl cri - ne que - sto cɔr, piɛn di ru - i - ne non ha
sue ca - te - ne, ma per cre - scer le mi - e pe - ne il pen -
2

Idiomatic translation: Tell me, Cupid, where has my freedom gone?

1) Since freedom left me, as you know, and tangled itself in a lovely head of hair, my poor desolated heart has not ever seen it again.

18
pɔi ri - vi - sta più. Dim - mi, a - mor, dim - mi che fa la mia
siɛr mai non tor - nɔ̀. Dim - mi, a - mor, dim - mi che fa la mia
cresc.
f
4 3
4 3

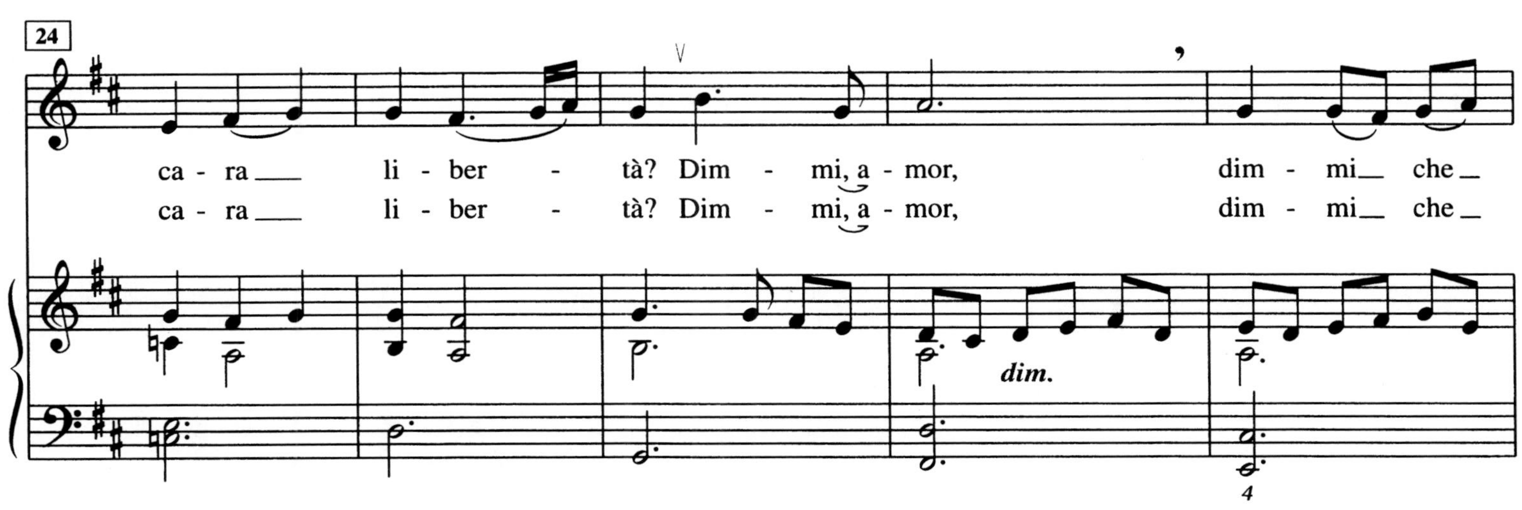
24
ca - ra li - ber - tà? Dim - mi, a - mor, dim - mi che
ca - ra li - ber - tà? Dim - mi, a - mor, dim - mi che
dim.
4

29
fa la mia ca - ra li - ber - tà?
fa la mia ca - ra li - ber - tà? 3. Quel pen - siɛr che
p

2) My heart sent out a thought to look for my freedom, where it is lying in chains, but to my greater pain, the thought never came back.

35
si par - tì re - stò__ for - se pri - gio - niɛ - ro, ch'in-na -

40
[mi fe -
mo - ra o - gni pen - siɛ - ro la bel - tà che mi fe -

45
rì.] [dim - mi]
rì. Dim - mi, a mor, dim - mi che fa il pen - siɛr,__ la__
cresc.
f

3) Perhaps the thought that left also remained a prisoner, because that beauty who wounded me bewitches every thought. Tell me, Cupid, what became of my thought? my freedom?

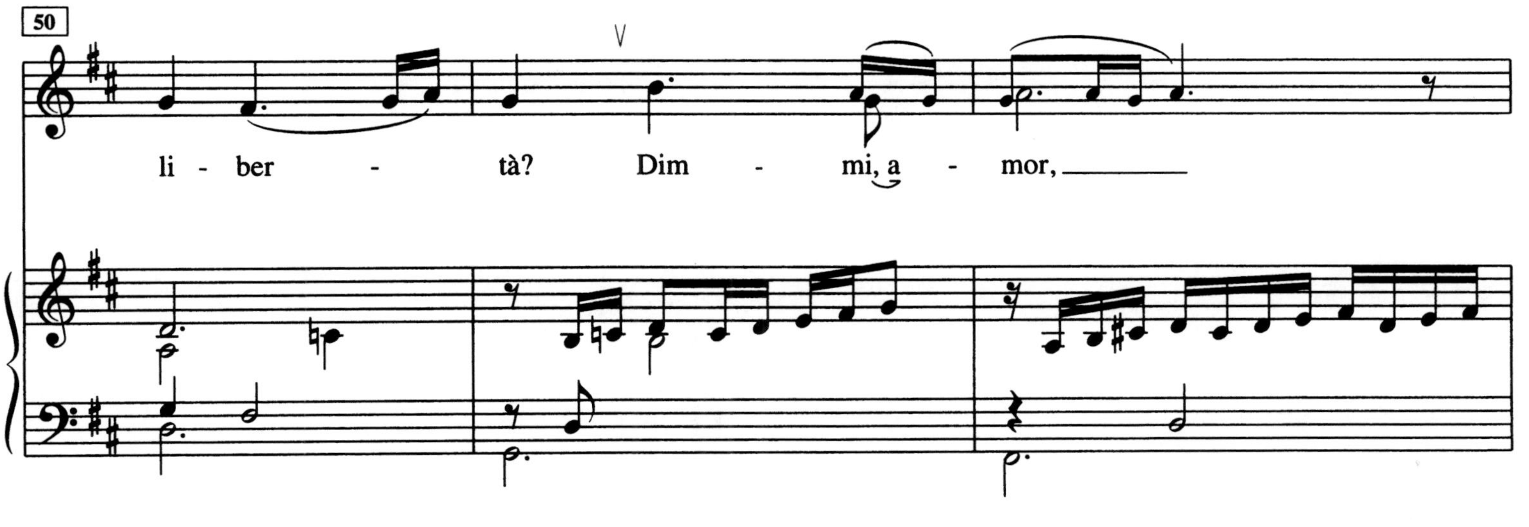
50
li - ber - tà? Dim - mi, a - mor,

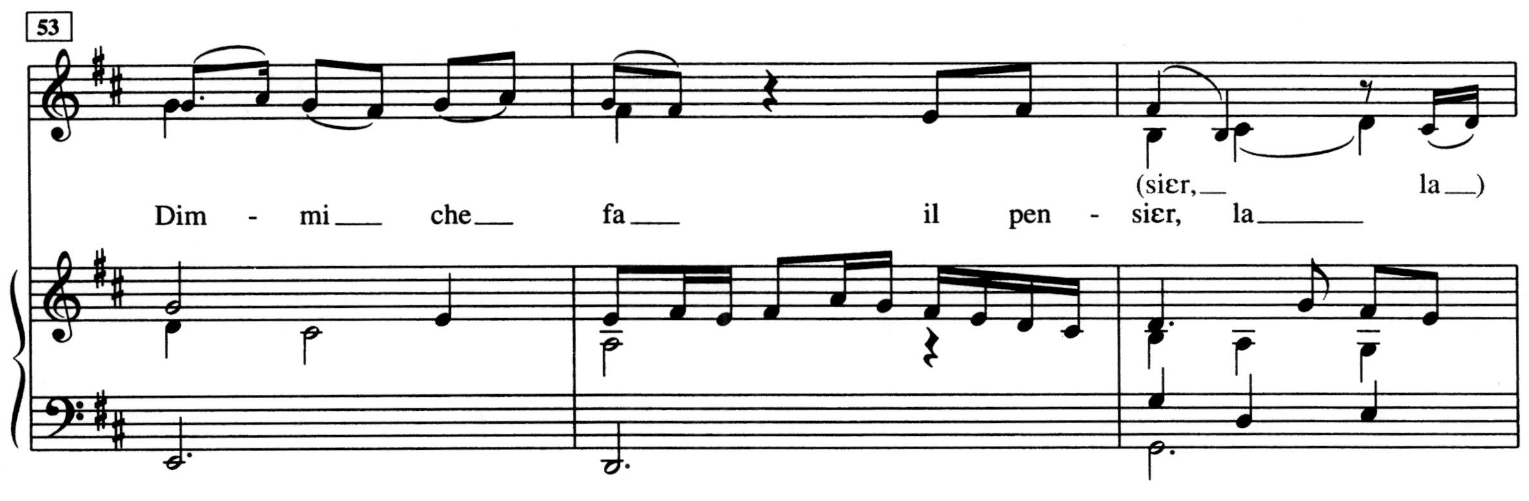
53
(siɛr, la)
Dim - mi che fa il pen - siɛr, la

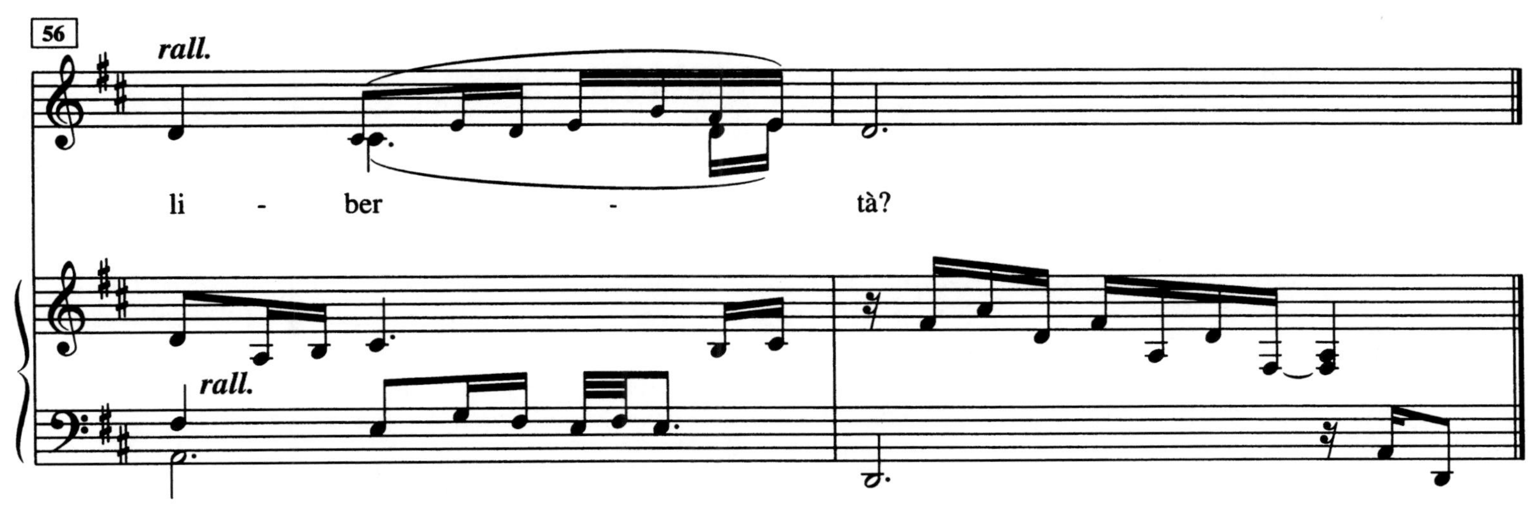
56
rall.
li - ber - tà?
rall.

Tu mancavi a tormentarmi

(Undated)

Carlo Caproli
[karlo kaprɔli]
(Rome, ca. 1617 – Rome, ca. 1692)

tu maŋkavi a tormentarmi
1 Tu mancavi a tormentarmi,
You omitted to torment-me,

krudelis:sima speɾantsa
2 Crudelissima speranza,
cruelest hope,

e kon doltʃe rimembrantsa
3 E con dolce rimembranza
and with sweet remembrance

pɔi di nwɔvo av:velenarmi
4 Poi di nuovo avvelenarmi.
then of new to-poison-myself.

aŋkor duɾa la zventuɾa
5 Ancor dura la sventura
Still lasts the misfortune

duna fjam:ma intʃeneɾita
6 D'una fiamma incenerita.
of-a flame turned-to-ash.

la feɾita aŋkoɾ apɛrta
7 La ferita ancor aperta
The wound still open

pur mav:vɛrta nwɔve pɛne
8 Pur m'avverta nuove pene.
indeed me-warns-about new pains.

dal rumor dɛl:le katɛne
9 Dal rumor delle catene
From-the noise of-the chains

mai non vedo al:lontanarmi
10 Mai non vedo allontanarmi.
ever not I-see distance-myself.

Poetic idea
"I was sadly disappointed in love, but time seemed to lessen the pain. Now I feel as if the wound is still open; the pain will never go away."

Background
Caproli, also called Caprioli, was such a fine violinist that he was often called "Carlo del Violino."

This is a fine early example of a *da capo aria*, a type that became enormously popular in later operas. The first section of a *da capo aria* is musically complete in itself; it begins and ends in the tonic key. The second section provides contrast by changing keys. In this case it also has a different meter. The first section then returns; usually this is indicated by the words *da capo* (from the top) written at the end of the second section. In this case a highly expressive transition (measures 52-54) prepares for the repetition.

Baroque theorists explained that a particular emotion can only be sustained for a limited time, and then it will be replaced naturally by another thought. After that one has been expressed, the first emotion can return with renewed force and freshness.

Because of its psychological validity, the repetitive aspect of da capo arias was viewed as an opportunity rather than as a problem. Singers used ornamentation as a means of contrast, assuring that the first part was not, in fact, repeated exactly.

Sources
(1) Ms. 2468, Biblioteca Casanatense, Rome. This leather-bound, gold-stamped volume contains 40 works by Carissimi, Rossi and other Roman composers. *"Tu mancavi"* is the second piece, occupying folios 13-26v. Attributed to Carlo del Violino. For voice (soprano clef) and continuo. Original key: C minor, signature of one flat. Meter: 3/2. Contains a second stanza, which begins *"Sempre intorno a chi m'uccida...."*
(2) Ms. Barb. lat. 4208, Biblioteca Apostolica Vaticana, Vatican City. This parchment-bound book, stamped with the Barberini family coat-of-arms, contains works by the same composers. No composer named for *"Tu mancavi,"* the second piece. Agrees with (1) in every detail and supplies a third stanza, which begins *"Ancor fuma il foco estinto...."*
(3) *D'autori romani musica volgare*, Vol. III, Civico Museo Bibliografico Musicale, Bologna, Ms. Q. 46. Composer: Carlo Caprioli. One stanza only.

The unusual rhythm of the first phrase is attested by all three sources. Also, the augmented harmony that is found in measures 22 and 77 is clearly indicated by the composer with the figures 6 and ♯3.

Gevaert, who based his version on a London manuscript, mistakenly named Antonio Cesti as the composer. Gevaert halved the note values in the first section, suggested a tempo of adagio, and used an accompaniment of repeated chords in Romantic style. At measure 12 instead of *"poi"* the word *"puoi"* (you-are-able) appears, probably incorrectly.

When Parisotti borrowed this aria from Gevaert, he simplified the rhythm of measure 1 and altered the questionable word *"puoi"* to *"vuoi"* (you-want).

Contrary to some references, this aria is not found in Cesti's opera *Orontea*.

Tu mancavi a tormentarmi

Poet unknown

Carlo Caproli
Realization by John Glenn Paton

Idiomatic translation: You stopped tormenting me, cruel hope,

and poisoning me again with sweet memories.

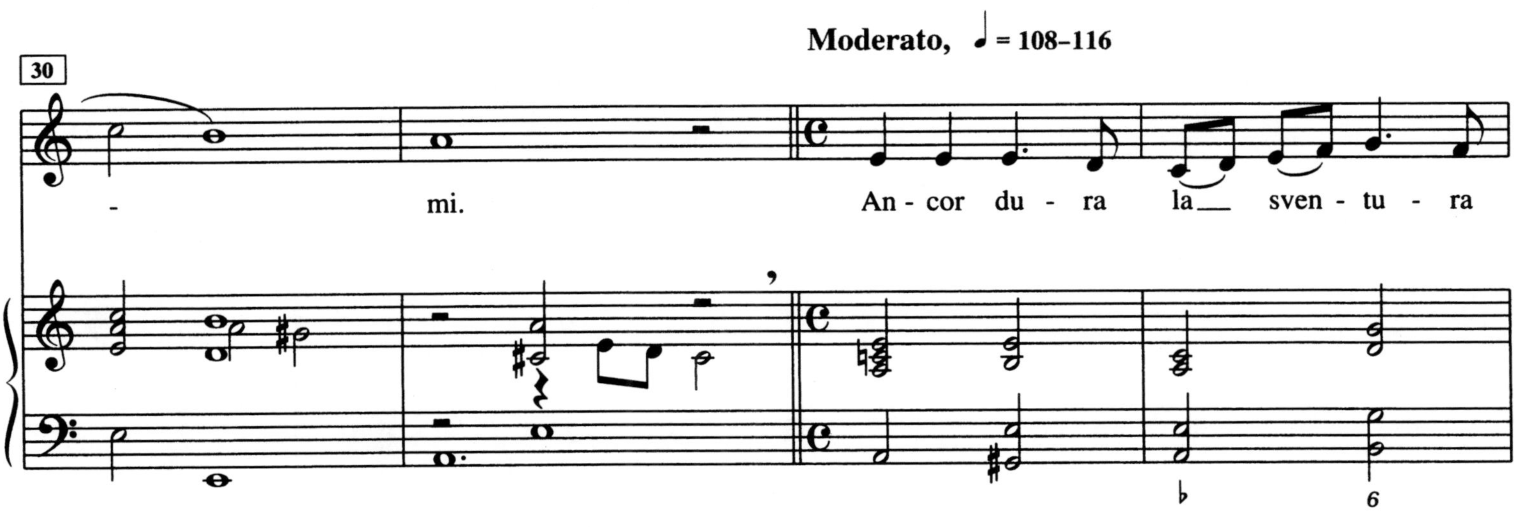

Still the misfortune lingers of a flame that has turned to ashes. The still-open wound

warns me about new pains. I never expect to escape from the sound of rattling chains.

50
rit.
ve - do al - lon - ta - nar - mi,
mai non ve - do al -
rit.
53
Tempo primo
lon - ta - nar - mi.
Tu man - ca -
57
tr
- vi a tor - men - tar - mi,
cru - de -
61
lis - si - ma spe - ran - za,

64
e con dol - ce ri - mem - bran - za pɔi di

68
nuɔ - vo av - ve - le - nar - mi, e con

72
dol - ce ri - mem - bran - za

76
poi di nuo - vo av - ve - le - nar - -

80
mi, poi di nuo - vo di nuo - vo av - ve - le -

84
nar - - - mi.
rit.

Si mantiene il mio amor

from "*Alessandro, vincitor di se stesso*" (1651)
[alesːsandro vintʃitor di se stesːso]

Antonio Cesti
[antɔnjo tʃɛsti]
(Arezzo, 1623 – Florence, 1669)

si mantjɛne
1 **Si mantiene**
Itself keeps-alive

il mio amor
2 **Il mio amor**
the my love

di dolor
3 **Di dolor,**
with grief,

dafːfanːni e pene
4 **D'affanni e pene,**
with-anxieties and pains

ke dʒoire del mio bɛne
5 **Che gioire del mio bene**
so-that to-be-happy about my beloved

nemː men pɔsːso kol pensjɛro
6 **Ne men posso col pensiero.**
nor less I-can with-the thought.

amo pur sebːbɛn non spɛro
7 **Amo pur, se ben non spero.**
I-love indeed, if well not I-hope.

Poetic idea
"My love brings me nothing but sadness, but I go on loving anyway." The singer is Efestione, a general in the army of Alexander the Great. The scene is Babylon in 331 B.C.E.*, where Alexander resides after defeating Darius III, King of Persia.

Efestione is in love with Campaspe, a famous beauty who was taken as a prisoner of war and given to Efestione to be his servant. He wants to marry her, but he is already committed to marry Cina, the sister of Alexander. Efestione is afraid to offend the sister of his powerful friend and king.

The story ends happily when it is revealed that Campaspe is Efestione's natural sister. When she was born, an astrologer predicted that her brother would fall in love with her; to prevent this her father sent her away to grow up in another country. Efestione embraces his new-found sister and happily returns to his former affection for Cina.

The opera is called *Alexander, Conqueror of Himself,* because of the self-control that Alexander shows at the end of the opera: he does not claim the beautiful Campaspe for himself, but gives her in marriage to a man whom she loves.

*Before Common Era

Background
The earliest operas were royal entertainments, lavish festivities for invited audiences. In 1637 Venice became the first city where public opera theaters would admit any person who was able to pay for a ticket. Backed financially by wealthy subscribers, Venetian opera was a popular entertainment and sometimes a profitable business, similar in many ways to the Broadway musical theater of the present.

Cesti was baptized as Pietro, but took the name Antonio when he became a Franciscan priest. (He was never Marc'Antonio as some books call him.) Although he was a priest, Cesti sang and toured as an operatic tenor. His successes onstage and in love affairs caused frequent reprimands from his religious superiors, and he was released from his vows in 1659.

Alessandro, Cesti's first opera, was composed for the Carnival season in Venice. Please read more about Cesti in the notes to *"Intorno all'idol mio"* (page 49).

Many kinds of musical symbolism appear in Baroque music, and this aria demonstrates some of them. Minor mode signifies both passion and sadness. The bass part is a "ground," a short melody that is repeated many times while other melodic lines develop freely above it. The downward scale tones of this ground symbolize sadness; repetition 13 times shows that the sadness is persistent and hopeless. Although there is not even a change of key to relieve the feeling of depression, the composer keeps the aria interesting with changing harmonies and with contrast between the voice and the two violins that accompany it. The phrase lengths are also irregular and unpredictable, so that variety in the vocal phrasing contrasts with the consistent phrasing in the bass part.

Sources
(1) *Alessandro*, manuscript score of the opera, Biblioteca Apostolica Vaticana, Rome, Chigi Q.V.61. Act II, scene 1. For voice (soprano clef), two violins (probably), and continuo. Original key: D minor (no signature).
(2) *Alessandro, vincitor di se stesso*, libretto, copy at University of California at Los Angeles, 1651,2.

This aria has not been published previously.

Si mantiene il mio amor

Francesco Sbarra

Antonio Cesti
Realization by John Glenn Paton

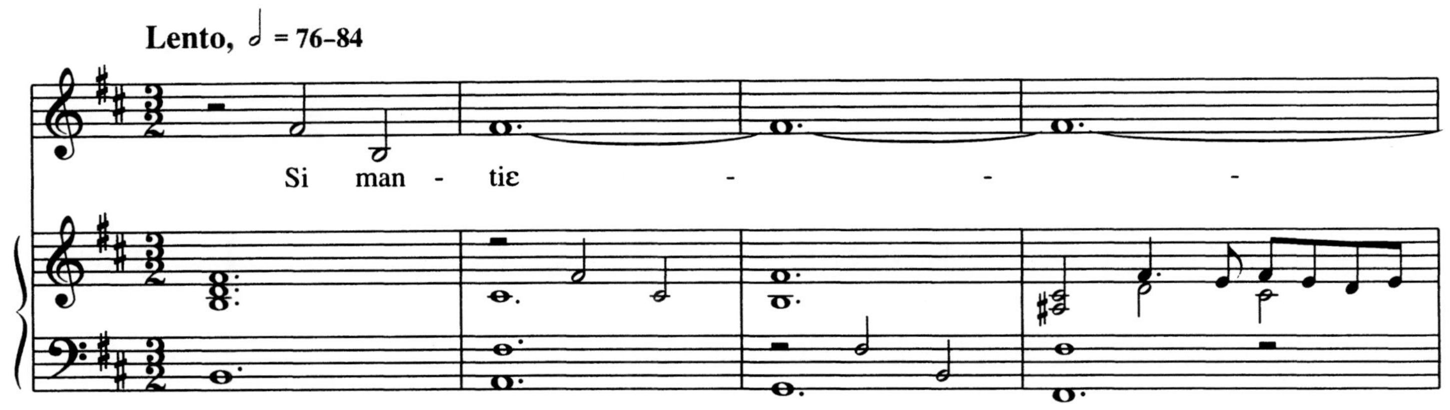

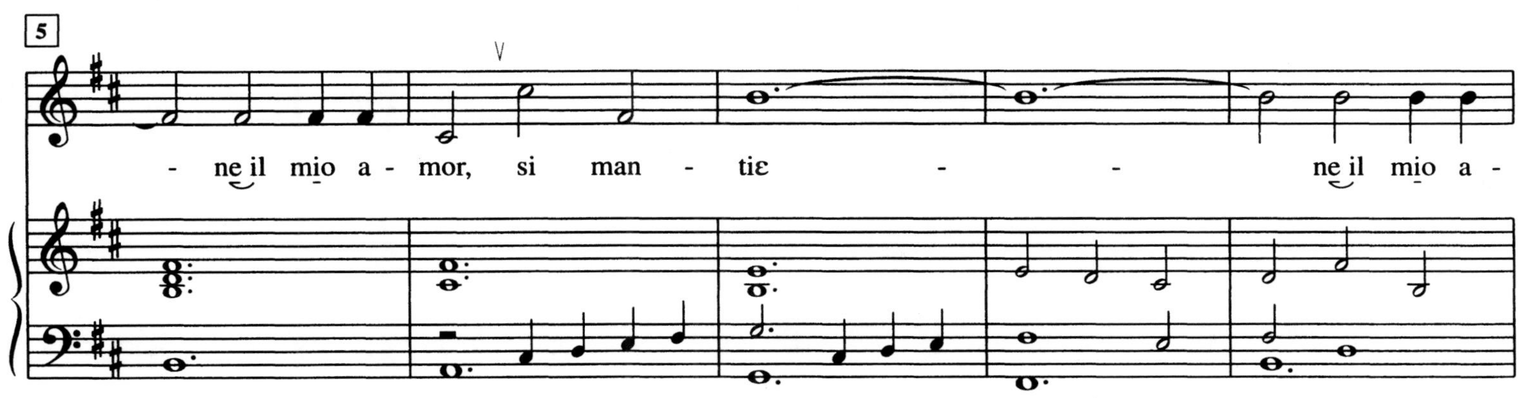

Idiomatic translation: My love is nourished by grief, anxiety and pain,

so much so that I cannot even be happy in thinking about my beloved.

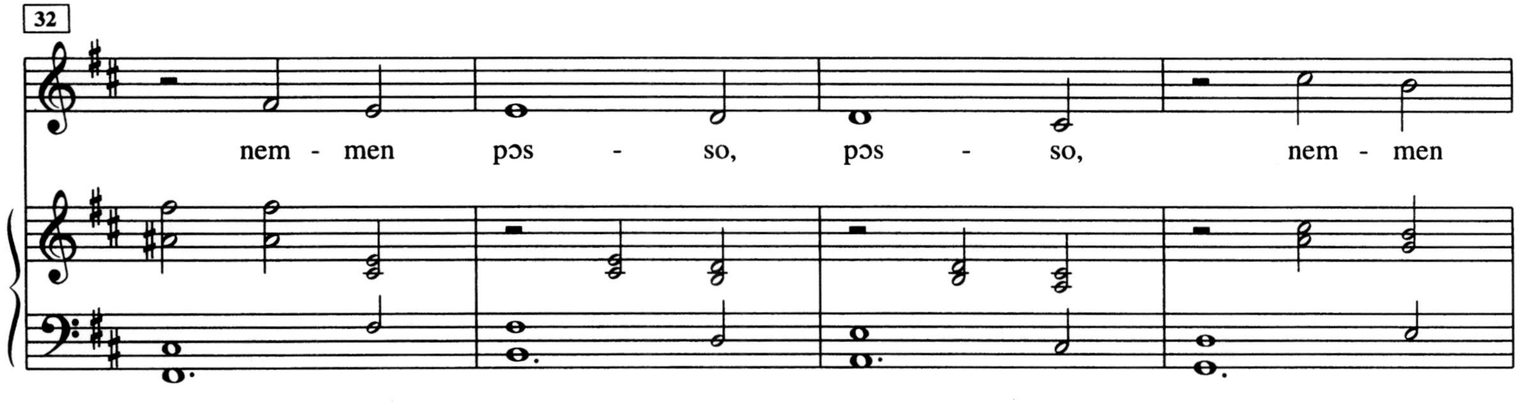

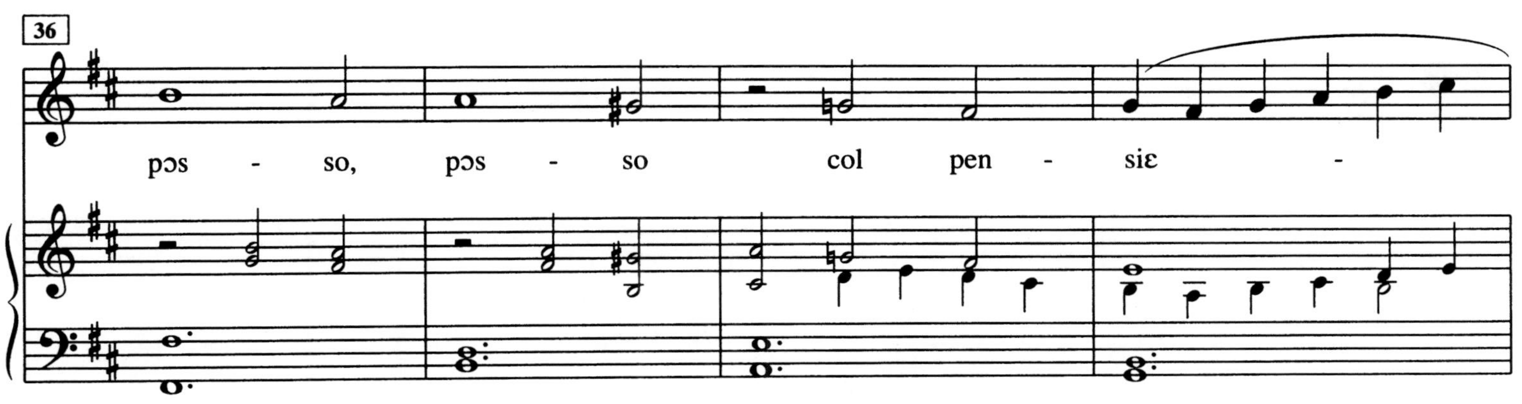

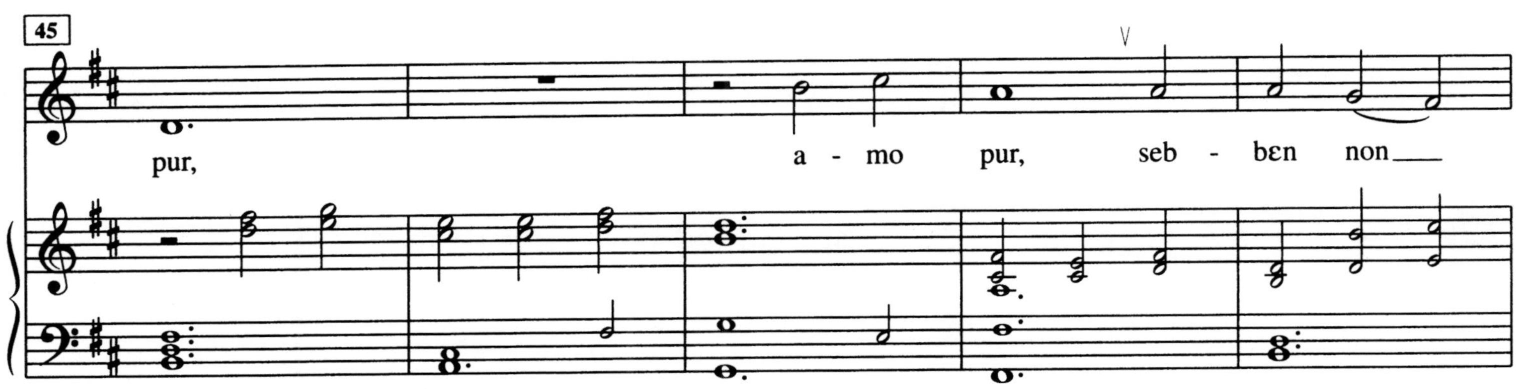

I love, however, even if I do not hope.

An excerpt showing measures 43-51 of *"Si mantiene il mio amor,"* slightly reduced. The two staves with G clefs are for violins. The third staff has a soprano clef (middle C on the lowest line) for the voice. The bass part has an F clef. The key is D Minor with no signature. Notice the lack of capitalization, punctuation, dynamics, and keyboard harmonization. Slurs are carelessly drawn and do not extend more than one measure.

Intorno all'idol mio

from *"Orontea"* (1656)
[orontɛa]

Antonio Cesti
[antɔnjo tʃɛsti]
(Arezzo, 1623 – Florence, 1669)

intorno al:lidol mio
1 Intorno all'idol mio
Around to-the-idol mine

spiɾate pur spiɾate
2 Spirate pur, spirate,
blow then, blow,

auɾe soavi e grate
3 Aure soavi e grate,
breezes gentle and pleasant,

e nel:le gwantʃe elɛt:te
4 E nelle guance elette
and on-the cheeks chosen

batʃatelo per me
5 Baciatelo per me,
kiss-him for me,

kortezi auɾet:te
6 Cortesi aurette.
courteous little-breezes.

al mio bɛn ke ripɔza
7 Al mio ben, che riposa
To my good, who reposes

sul:lali del:la kwjɛte
8 Sull'ali della quiete,
on-the-wings of calm,

grati sɔɲ:ɲi as:sistete
9 Grati sogni assistete,
pleasant dreams be-present,

el mio rak:kjuzo ardoɾe
10 E'l mio racchiuso ardore
and-the my held-in ardor

zvelateʎ:ʎi per me
11 Svelategli per me,
reveal-to-him for me

larve damoɾe
12 Larve d'amore.
spirits of-love.

Poetic idea
"May my love sleep in peace and enjoy pleasant dreams." The singer is Orontea, the (fictitious) Queen of Egypt.

Orontea is alone with her beloved Alidoro, who is asleep. Her counselors forbid her to marry him, because he is a commoner. The opera ends happily with the discovery that Alidoro is really of royal birth and worthy to marry a queen.

Cicognini was a successful writer of dozens of stage comedies and four opera libretti. His libretto for *Orontea*, or with its full title *The Chaste Loves of Orontea*, was set to music by three other composers after Cesti.

The text could be sung to either a male or a female beloved. The words *idol* and *ben* often refer to a woman, even though they are grammatically masculine.

Background
Cesti composed *Orontea* at Innsbruck, Austria, where he was employed at the court of the archduke, 1652-1657. The opera was well received and was revived by various opera companies into the 1680s.

Cesti later served as court composer in Vienna, where he wrote one of the most massive operas in history: *Il pomo d'oro (The Golden Apple)*, in a prologue and five acts.

A close friend of Cesti's was Salvator Rosa, a famous painter and writer. This aria is the first piece in a hand-written music book that once belonged to Rosa. It was later bought by Charles Burney, who included this aria as a musical example in *A General History of Music* (1776).

Sources
(1) *I casti amori d'Orontea*, manuscript score of the opera, Biblioteca Apostolica Vaticana, Rome, Chigi Q.V.53. In Act II, scene 17. For voice (soprano clef), two violins and continuo. Original key: E minor.
(2) Manuscript collection, formerly Salvator Rosa's, Bibliothèque Nationale, Paris, Rés. Vmc ms. 78.

The unusual melodic variations in the second stanza are original, not added by the editor.

In this edition the violin parts and continuo are printed normally; smaller noteheads are used for added harmony tones. In measures 1-7 and 36-41 the first violin part is lowered an octave to put it below the second violin, which has the more important melody.

Orontea had its first modern performances at Cornell University, Ithaca, New York, conducted by William C. Holmes. His edition of the score (without keyboard realization) was published by Wellesley College, 1973. The introduction describes four existing manuscript scores of the opera and provides a scene by scene synopsis. Much of the information given above comes from Dr. Holmes.

Banck's romanticized arrangement of this aria shows no awareness of the original violin parts. This is one of altogether eleven songs that Parisotti borrowed from Banck.

Intorno all'idol mio

Giacinto Andrea Cicognini

Antonio Cesti
Realization by John Glenn Paton

Idiomatic translation: Around my beloved, breathe gently, sweet and pleasing breezes,

and kiss his (her) dear cheeks, courteous breezes.

Pleasant dreams, visit my beloved, who reposes on wings of quietness.

Visions of love, reveal my hidden love to him (her) on my behalf.

70
tr
- ve d'a - mo - re.

74

78

In amor ci vuol ardir

(Undated)

Antonia Bembo
[antɔnja bɛmbo]
(Venice, ca. 1640 – Paris, ca. 1715)

in amor tʃi vwɔl ardir
1 **In amor ci vuol ardir,**
In love, there must-be burning,

trɔpːpo timido mio kɔr
2 **Troppo timido mio cor!**
too timid my heart!

skatːʃa omai skatːʃa il timor
3 **Scaccia omai, scaccia il timor**
Drive-out always, drive-out the fear

se tu brami di dʒoir
4 **Se tu brami di gioir.**
if you desire to rejoice.

Poetic idea
"Let go, be courageous, if you want to be happy in love!"

Aurelia Fedeli (ca. 1613-1704), an Italian actress and poet, came to France as a member of a *commedia dell'arte* troupe in the 1640s. She settled in France and published two books of poetry and drama for the French court in the 1660s; Louis XIV's mother, Queen Anne of Austria, rewarded Fedeli's talent with royal gifts. In 1685, around the time of her retirement from the stage, Fedeli became a naturalized French citizen, changing her name to Brigide Fidèle. Many of her poems were set to music by such well-known composers as Cavalli and Steffani.

Background
Antonia Bembo, born Antonia Padoani, studied with Cavalli in her youth. She married Lorenzo Bembo, a Venetian nobleman, in 1659 and had three children. For reasons that are now unknown, she left her family in circa 1676 and went to France. Her singing and her creative abilities so impressed King Louis XIV that he awarded her a pension, enabling her to live in a women's religious community in Paris. There she composed a considerable quantity of sacred and secular music in Italian, French and Latin. Her only dated work is an Italian opera, *Ercole amante* (1707).

"In amor ci vuol ardir" comes from Bembo's first volume of music, *Produzioni armoniche*. Based on the occasions for which some of the pieces were composed, this volume can be dated circa 1697. At that time Fedeli and Bembo were neighbors in the parish of Notre Dame de Bonne Nouvelle in Paris.

Apparently the two artistic women were well acquainted, and Fedeli personally gave some poems to Bembo. *"In amor ci vuol ardir"* is one of a group of three settings of Fedeli poems, all unique to this volume and published nowhere else.

Source
Produzioni Armoniche, a manuscript collection, almost certainly the composer's autograph, Bibliothèque Nationale, Paris, Rés.Vm^1 117, pp. 160-162. For voice (soprano clef) and continuo. Original key: A minor. The somewhat illogical meter signature is 8/6.

The volume, 21 cm. high by 28.5 cm. wide, is handsomely bound in red leather stamped with gold. The decorations include the fleur-de-lis, an emblem of French royalty. The poet is identified in the table of contents.

Long slurs are all editorial; Bembo never extended a slur over more than three notes. Accidentals are placed inconsistently; it is often doubtful whether the sixth and seventh scale degrees should be raised or not.

It is difficult to know how Bembo intended the words to match the notes. For instance, the first two lines of the text are identical in length but the first two phrases of the melody are not. Bembo wrote slurs inconsistently: sometimes clearly and deliberately, at other times so carelessly that one can only guess which notes are included. If some of my interpretations seem awkward or difficult to sing, one may change them freely.

The first public performance of this aria was given by David Parks, tenor, and Joan Thompson, pianist, in Fairbanks, AK, in 1993.

My thanks to Dr. Claire Fontijn of Wellesley College, who brought Bembo's music to my attention and generously supplied the biographical information given above. For more details, see her dissertation: *Antonia Bembo: "les gouts réunis," royal patronage, and the role of the woman composer during Louis XIV's reign.*

In amor ci vuol ardir

Aurelia Fedeli

Antonia Bembo
Realization by John Glenn Paton

Idiomatic translation: In love, one must burn, poor timid heart of mine!

Drive out fear if you ever want to be happy.

15
mor se tu bra - - - mi
6
17
di gio - ir.
19
Scac - cia o - ma - i, scac-cia il ti - mor se
21
tu bra - mi di gio - ir, se tu bra - mi di gio -
4
3
6
6♯
6
4
3

23
ir, se tu bra - - - mi,
25
se tu bra - mi di gio -
27
ir, se tu bra - - - mi,
29
se tu bra - mi di gio - ir!

Toglietemi la vita

from *Pompeo* (1683)
[pompɛo]

Alessandro Scarlatti
[alesːsandro skarlatːti]
(Palermo, 1660 – Naples, 1725)

toʎːʎetemi la vita aŋkor
1 **Toglietemi la vita ancor,**
Take-from-me the life again,

krudɛli
2 **Crudeli**
cruel

tʃɛli
3 **Cieli,**
heavens,

se mi volete rapire il kɔr
4 **Se mi volete rapire il cor.**
if from-me you-want to-remove the heart.

negatemi i rai del di
5 **Negatemi i rai del dì,**
Deny-for-me the eyes of day,

sevɛre
6 **Severe**
stern

sfɛre
7 **Sfere,**
spheres,

se vage sjɛte del mio dolor
8 **Se vaghe siete del mio dolor.**
if eager you-are for my sorrow.

Poetic idea
"If I cannot regain my lost love, let me die!" The singer is Mitridate, formerly the king of Pontus. The scene is Rome sometime after 65 B.C.E., when the Roman general Pompey the Great (in Italian Pompeo) conquered Pontus. He has brought the queen of Pontus to Rome as a captive. Mitridate comes to Rome in disguise to look for his wife. When he sings this aria, he has not yet found her, and he despairs of ever seeing her again.

The first version of this opera was written by librettist Nicolò Minato and composer Francesco Cavalli in Venice in 1666. In typical Venetian fashion, Minato's plot included the comic antics of servants. To suit the tastes of the Roman audience in 1683, an anonymous revisor deleted the comic scenes and added more serious aria texts, supposedly from other works by Minato. These include the two arias in this volume.

In the second stanza it is advisable to separate the two words *"negatemi i."* Usually, two identical vowels merge with each other in Italian, but here the energy of the rhythm implies a slight separation.

Background
Scarlatti was 22 years old when he wrote *Pompeo*, his fourth opera. He and his wife Antonia already had three sons and expected their fourth child.

Scarlatti was music director to Queen Christina of Sweden, who was exiled from her Lutheran country because of her conversion to Catholicism. She was an avid patron of the arts and a leader of Roman society, but she was not rich enough to build her own theater. *Pompeo* was performed at the private theater of the Colonna family.

Measures 6 and 14 contain excellent examples of a harmony that is especially associated with Neapolitan music, using the lowered second tone of the scale.

Another famous aria from *Pompeo* is *"O cessate di piagarmi,"* found in *26 Italian Songs and Arias.*

Source
Pompeo, Act I, scene 4. Manuscript score of the opera in the Bibliothèque royale Albert Ier., Brussels, MS II 3962. For voice (tenor clef), two violins, viola and continuo. Original key: C minor (signature of two flats). Meter: C. Photo-reproduction in *Handel Sources*, Vol. 6 (New York: Garland, 1986).

In this edition the string orchestra parts are shown by larger noteheads, the editor's continuo realization by smaller noteheads.

This aria has been published by many editors from the mid-1800s up to recent editions by Knud Jeppesen and Luigi Dallapiccola. None of them used sources that include the vigorously contrapuntal string parts.

Toglietemi la vita

Nicolò Minato

Alessandro Scarlatti (1660–1725)
Realization by John Glenn Paton

Idiomatic translation: 1) Take away my life, cruel heavens, if you want to take away my love.

2) Take away the light of the day, severe stars, if you are eager to make me unhappy.

14
to - glie - te - mi,
to - glie - te - mi, to - glie - te - mi la vi - ta an -
to - glie - te - mi la vi - ta an -
16
p
cor, to - glie - te - mi la vi - ta an cor.
cor, to - glie - te - mi la vi - ta an cor.
a
p
f
19
1.
2.
Ne - ga - te - mi i rai del
1.
2.

ⓐ If an introduction is desired, begin here.

Amor preparami

from *Pompeo* (1683)
[pompɛo]

Alessandro Scarlatti
alesːsandro skarlatːti
(Palermo, 1660 – Naples, 1725)

amor preparami
1 Amor, preparami
Love, prepare-for-me

altre katene
2 Altre catene,
other chains,

ovːvero laʃːʃami
3 Ovvero lasciami
or-truly leave-me

in liberta
4 In libertà.
in liberty.

io vɔ tʃertisːsimo
5 Io vò certissimo
I want most-certainly

kwel nɔdo frandʒere
6 Quel nodo frangere
that knot to-break

kin latːʃo asprisːsimo
7 Ch'in laccio asprissimo
which-in tie most-harsh

stretːto mi tjɛne
8 Stretto mi tiene
tight me holds

sɛntsa pjeta
9 Senza pietà.
without pity.

Poetic idea
"Let me find some other love, or perhaps none at all! The love I am in now is hopeless!" The singer is Claudio, son of Julius Caesar.

The scene is Rome sometime after 65 B.C.E., when Pompey the Great, for whom the opera is named, conquered Pontus. Pompey has brought Queen Issicratea of Pontus to Rome as a captive. At this point in the opera, Issicratea's husband has come to Rome in disguise to rescue her. She has seen him and hopes to be reunited with him. Claudio does not know this and does not understand why she rejects his offer of love.

You may read more about the opera in the notes that precede *"Toglietemi la vita"* (page 60)

Background
Except for a few romantic comedies in exotic settings, the stories of Scarlatti's operas are all derived from ancient Roman history. His aristocratic patrons wanted idealized stories about persons of nobility caught in rivalries of love and conflicts between love and duty. They never imagined operas about contemporary problems, and in any case the government censors would not have permitted such stories onstage.

Musically, Scarlatti's operas consisted for the most part of recitatives alternating with arias. Recitatives are used to carry on conversations and convey information. Although they are always in 4/4 meter, they employ irregular, non-repetitive rhythms like those of speech. An aria occurs when the action of the story stops and the character takes time to express a personal emotion. Arias have regular, dance-like rhythms and as much melodic expressiveness as the composer can achieve.

Source
Pompeo, Act I, scene 8. Manuscript score of the opera in the Bibliothèque royale Albert Ier., Brussels, MS II 3962. For voice (soprano clef) and continuo. Original key: F major (no signature). Meter: 3/4 (most measures contain six quarter notes). A ritornello for strings follows the aria.

Handel knew this opera and used parts of ten arias in various works of his own. He quoted from *"Amor preparami"* in the chorus "To him your grateful notes" in the oratorio *Hercules* (1744). The Brussels score is the only one known to survive and probably was the score that Handel owned. A photo reproduction of it has been published in *Handel Sources*, Vol. 6 (New York: Garland, 1986), edited by John H. Roberts.

This aria has not been published in any previous anthology.

Amor preparami

Nicolò Minato

Alessandro Scarlatti
Realization by John Glenn Paton

Idiomatic translation: Love, prepare some other chains for me, or else let me be free.

I desire firmly to break that knot which with harsh sternness holds me pitilessly.

39
mf
pa - ra - mi,
a - mor, pre - pa - ra - mi
mf
44
p
cresc.
f
al - tre ca - te - - - ne ov - ve - ro
p
cresc.
f
49
tr
la - scia - mi in li - ber - tà, in li - ber -
53
tr
tà, ov - ve - ro la - scia - mi in li - ber - tà.

Deh, più à me non v'ascondete

from *Eraclea* (1692)
[eɾaklɛa]

Giovanni Bononcini
[dʒovanːni bonontʃini]
(Modena, 1670 – Vienna, 1747)

dɛ pju a me non vaskondete
1 **Deh, più à me non v'ascondete**
Please, more to me not yourselves-hide,

lutʃi vage del mio sol
2 **Luci vaghe del mio sol.**
lights lovely of my sun.

kon zvelarvi se voi sjɛte
3 **Con svelarvi, se voi siete,**
With revealing-yourselves, if you are,

voi potete
4 **Voi potete**
you can

trar kwɛstalma fwɔr di dwɔl
5 **Trar quest'alma fuor di duol.**
draw this-soul away from sorrow.

Poetic idea
"Please look at me. That's all I need to make me happy." The singer is Mirena, a Sabine noblewoman, in the opera *Eraclea, or The Abduction of the Sabine Women*.

Legend tells that when the early Romans had a shortage of women, they abducted the women from a neighboring tribe, the Sabines. Mirena is one of the abducted women. Her husband has come in disguise, looking for her and hoping to recapture her from the Romans. Mirena believes she recognizes her husband, but he is afraid to admit his identity even to her.

Background
The story of the Sabine women was made into an opera at Vienna in 1674 by two Italians who were prominent at the Austrian court, librettist Nicolò Minato and composer Antonio Draghi.

When Draghi's opera was revived in 1692 at the Tordinona Theater in Rome, the impresario decided that more arias were needed. He engaged a new librettist, Stampiglia, and a 21-year-old composer, Bononcini, to supply them.

Giovanni Bononcini was the son of a well-known composer and theorist, Giovanni Maria Bononcini. Orphaned at an early age, Giovanni and his younger brother Antonio matured musically in Bologna. Giovanni arrived in Rome during one of the periods when the ecclesiastical government tolerated public performances of operas. When the theater closed soon after, he found employment in the wealthy Colonna household.

Bononcini often spelled his name "Buononcini." Some older publications wrongly gave him a middle name "Battista."

Another aria from the same opera is *"Non posso disperar,"* found in *26 Italian Songs and Arias*.

Sources
No score of the opera in Bononcini's version exists. There are three manuscript sources for this aria, all in the handwriting of the same professional copyist:
(1) *Arie della commedia del ratto delle sabbine*, Biblioteca apostolica vaticana, Vatican City, Barberini latini 4161;
(2) no title, same library, Barberini latini 4164;
(3) no title, Biblioteca musicale governativa del Conservatorio di Musica "S. Cecilia," Rome, G 392.
(4) Libretto, *Eraclea*, Biblioteca Estense, Modena, 70.E.10, Act 2, scene 11. Probably from the Rome production, but there is no date nor the name of either composer or librettist.
(5) *Il ratto delle Sabine* by Antonio Draghi, manuscript score of the opera, Österreichische Nationalbibliothek, Vienna, Leopoldina 16291. The scene between Mirena and Mezio takes place in recitative only; Mirena does not sing an aria.

Manuscripts (1), (2) and (3) all confirm that the composer was Bononcini. For voice (soprano clef) and continuo. Original key: A major (signature of two sharps).

In the continuo realization chords have been left incomplete at times when the voice is resolving a suspension, for instance, in the third measure, third beat. Later composers would have doubled the voice, but a rare, written realization by Alessandro Scarlatti shows that he preferred not to have the keyboard player double the voice. This practice is assumed to be valid for Bononcini as well.

Parisotti, working from source (3), wrongly attributed the aria to Bononcini's father.

Deh, più a me non v'ascondete

Silvio Stampiglia

Giovanni Bononcini
Realization by John Glenn Paton

Largo, ♩ = 42–46
Dεh, più a me non v'a - scon -

4
de - te, lu - ci va - ghe del mio sol,

6
dεh, più a me non v'a - scon - de - te, lu - ci va - ghe del mio
2

Idiomatic translation: Please do not hide yourselves, lovely eyes.

8
sol, lu - ci va-ghe del mio sol, lu-ci va - ghe del mio

10
sol, lu - ci va-ghe del mio sol,

12
Con sve - lar - vi, se voi siε - te, voi po - te - te trar que-
2

By revealing yourselves, if it is really you, you can take away my sadness.

15
st'al - ma fuɔr di duɔl. Voi po - te - te trar que-st'al - ma fuɔr di

17
duɔl, trar que-st'al-ma fuɔr di duɔl.

20
Dɛh, più a me non v'a-scon - de - te, lu-ci va-ghe del mio sol,

23
deh, più a me non v'a - scon - de - te, lu - ci va - ghe del mio

25
sol, lu - ci va-ghe del mio sol, lu-ci va - ghe del mio

27
rit.
sol, lu - ci va-ghe del mio sol.
rit.

L'esperto nocchiero

from *Astarto* (1715)
[astarto]

Giovanni Bononcini
[dʒovan:ni bonontʃini]
(Modena, 1670 – Vienna, 1747)

lesperto nok:kjɛro
1 L'esperto nocchiero,
The-expert ship's-pilot

perke torna al lido
2 Perché torna al lido
why does-he-return to-the shore

ap:pena parti
3 Appena partì?
hardly set-sail?

del vɛnto kandʒato
4 Del vento cangiato,
Of-the wind changed,

del flut:to turbato
5 Del flutto turbato
of-the current stirred-up

sak:kɔrse fud:ʒi
6 S'accorse e fuggì.
he-took-note and fled.

sil mar luziŋgjɛro
7 S'il mar lusinghiero
If-the sea alluring

sapea kɛra infido
8 Sapea ch'era infido,
he-knew that-it-was unfaithful,

perke mai salpɔ
9 Perché mai salpò?
Why ever did-he-set-sail?

salpɔ ma iŋgan:nato
10 Salpò, ma ingannato
He-set-sail, but, betrayed,

al lido laʃ:ʃato
11 Al lido lasciato
to-the shore left-behind

in brɛve tornɔ
12 In breve tornò.
in a-short-time he-returned.

Poetic idea
"Why would a wise person change plans so quickly? Because conditions have changed and a quick response is needed." The singer is Nino, a minor character in the opera *Astarto*.

Nino has just promised Queen Elisa that he will commit a murder at her request because he believes that he will be rewarded with the hand of Sidonia, the woman he loves. The murder does not take place, and all ends happily.

Paolo Rolli (1687 - 1765) first met Bononcini in Rome, but also worked with him later in London. He was the poet of *"Se tu m'ami,"* which is found in *26 Italian Songs and Arias*.

Background
After beginning his career successfully in Rome, Bononcini worked for fourteen years in Vienna, where he composed twenty operas. He then returned to Rome in the service of the Viennese ambassador, and there he produced *Astarto* early in 1715.

When Bononcini arrived in London to compose operas for the Royal Academy of Music, he was a distinguished gentleman of fifty and his music was known throughout Europe. He chose *Astarto* for his first production in London on November 19, 1720, at King's Theater. *Astarto* ran for twenty-four performances that season, a record never equalled by Bononcini's younger competitor, George Frideric Handel (1685-1759).

According to a custom of the Baroque era, this aria should sound as if it were written in 12/8 meter: when triplets are present, a dotted eighth and sixteenth should be performed as if they were a quarter and eighth in compound meter.

Sources
(1) *Astartus*, Act 3, no. 5. Published score of the overture and arias (London: Walsh, no date), Bibliothèque nationale, Paris, two copies, D.1528(1) and Vm760, page 65. For voice (treble clef), two violins and continuo. Original key: B-flat major.
(2) Libretto, Huntington Library, San Marino, Cal., 50530. Act III, scene 3.

The first stanza of this aria has an unusual texture: the voice is doubled by unison violins with support from the continuo only at cadences. Because unison doubling by a piano will not have the same effect, this edition doubles the melody one octave lower and adds a light harmonization.

The second stanza has a different accompaniment: Violin I doubles the voice; Violin II plays an independent part; violas and cellos play the bass part, but *"senza cembalo"* (without the chordal support of the harpsichord).

The numerous repeat markings may be regarded as optional.

This aria was edited by Pietro Floridia (Philadelphia: Oliver Ditson, 1924) with a piano accompaniment in bravura style. As a tempo Floridia suggested *andante un poco mosso*.

L'esperto nocchiero

Paolo Antonio Rolli

Giovanni Bononcini
Realization by John Glenn Paton

Idiomatic translation: "Why is that expert sailor putting back to shore when he only just set sail?"

The wind has changed, the sea is turbulent; he took notice and returned. "If the alluring sea was always treacherous,

why did he ever set sail?" He set sail, but, being betrayed, he returned at once.

31

pace ſi moſtraal mio cor affanno che piace mi viene a bear mi viene a bear

An excerpt showing measures 12-20 of *"Un'ombra di pace."*

Un'ombra di pace

from *Calfurnia* (1724)
[kalfurnia]

Giovanni Bononcini
[dʒovanːni bonontʃini]
(Modena, 1670 – Vienna, 1747)

unombra di patʃe
1 Un'ombra di pace
A-shadow of peace

si mostra al mio kɔr
2 Si mostra al mio cor.
itself shows to my heart.

afːfanːno ke pjatʃe
3 Affanno che piace
Anxiety that pleases

mi vjɛne a bear
4 Mi viene a bear.
me comes to bless.

mi par ke si kandʒi
5 Mi par che si cangi
To-me seems that itself changes

in dʒɔja il dolor
6 In gioia il dolor,
into joy the sorrow,

e dika tu pjandʒi
7 E dica: tu piangi
and says, "You weep,

ma devi speɾar
8 Ma devi sperar.
but you-should hope.

Poetic idea
"Something good is about to happen." The singer is Giulia, the mother of Calfurnia, for whom the opera is named. In addition to being the wife of the Roman consul Gaius Marius, Giulia (Julia) is also a member of the renowned family of the Caesars and the aunt of Julius Caesar.

The Roman historian Plutarch records that in 101 B.C.E. Gaius Marius went into battle against an invading Germanic tribe. He received a message from an oracle that he could only win if he would sacrifice a member of his family to the gods. He assumed that this meant the death of his daughter, and agreed to the sacrifice.

The opera also has subplots driven by various jealousies. In Act III, Giulia saves her husband from an attempted murder and immediately realizes that if he goes on living, her daughter must die. Seizing on the idea of heavenly justice as her only hope, Giulia sings this aria about her hope that Calfurnia will somehow be saved.

Indeed, the opera reaches a happy ending, and Calfurnia does not die. Marius had received a false interpretation of the oracle from a cousin who was angry because he was not allowed to marry Calfurnia. Ironically, when the cousin dies, the oracle is satisfied, and Marius goes off to victory.

The first version of *Calfurnia* was written by librettist Grazio Braccioli and German composer Johann David Heinichen in Venice (1713). The libretto was adapted for Handel by Nicola Haym (1678-1729), who added the text of this aria. Haym was an Italian cellist and composer who wrote librettos for both Handel and Bononcini.

Background
Bononcini came to London in 1720 in the service of an opera company called the Royal Academy of Music. The musical director of the company was Handel, who had studied in Italy and also wrote superb Italian operas. In Bononcini's first two seasons in London his operas were performed 63 times, Handel's only 28 times. Neither composer ever publicly voiced an opinion of the other's music, but the public saw them as rivals and competitors. The following "Epigram on the Feuds Between Handel and Bononcini" by John Byrom concludes that they were more alike than different:

Some say, compar'd to Bononcini,
That Mynheer Handel's but a Ninny;
Others aver, that he to Handel
Is scarcely fit to hold a candle:
Strange all this Difference should be
'Twixt Tweedle-dum and Tweedle-dee!

After a year off, Bononcini was reengaged in the fall of 1723, and *Calfurnia* was premiered on April 18, 1724. Later that year Bononcini entered the service of the Duchess of Marlborough and subsequently wrote only one more opera for the London stage.

Sources
(1) *Apollo's Feast*, a collection of popular arias from many Italian operas (London: Walsh, [1726]), copy in Bibliothèque Nationale, Paris, Vm3.216bis, pp. 214-215. For voice (G clef), two violins, viola and continuo. Original key: B♭ major.
(2) Libretto in Italian and English, University of Chicago, PQ4684. B64C2.

In this edition six measures of music have been omitted following measure 37. The same music appears in the postlude, measures 95-100.

This aria has never appeared in an anthology.

Un'ombra di pace

Nicola Haym

Giovanni Bononcini
Realization by John Glenn Paton

Tempo giusto (Vivace), ♩ = 126–140

5

10

Un' om - bra di pa - ce si mo - stra al mi - o cɔr. Af - fan - no che

16

pia - ce mi viɛ - ne a be - ar, mi viɛ - ne a be - ar. [Ah!

Idiomatic translation: A foretaste of peace appears to my heart. A worry turned into pleasure is coming to bless me.

It seems to me that sorrow is turning into joy,

while saying to me, "You are weeping, but you ought to take hope."

64
mo - stra al mi - o cɔr. Af - fan - no che pia - ce mi viɛ - ne a be -
69
ar, mi viɛ - ne a be - ar. [Ah!
74
] Un'
79
om - bra di pa - ce si mo - stra al mio cɔr. Af -

83
rit.
tr
fan - no che pia - ce mi viε - ne a be - ar.
rit.
a tempo

87

92
tr

Selve amiche

from *La costanza in amor vince l'inganno* (1710)
[la kostantsa in amor vintʃe liŋganːno]

Antonio Caldara
[antɔnjo kaldara]
(Venice, ca. 1670 – Vienna, 1736

selve amike ombroze pjante
1 Selve amiche, ombrose piante,
Woods friendly, shady trees,

fido albɛrgo del mio kɔre
2 Fido albergo del mio core,
faithful shelter of my heart

kjɛde a voi kwestalma amante
3 Chiede a voi quest'alma amante
asks of you this-soul loving

kwalke patʃe al suo dolore
4 Qualche pace al suo dolore.
some peace for its sadness.

Poetic idea
"I come to the woods looking for some consolation for my broken heart." The singer is Silvia, a shepherdess.

This aria opens the opera entitled *Constancy in Love Defeats Treachery*. In the following scene Silvia tells a shepherd, Aminta, that she no longer loves him because she has fallen in love with Tirsi. Aminta then sings *"Sebben, crudele."* (See *26 Italian Songs and Arias*, page 84.)

Background
Caldara grew up in Venice, where he was a choirboy at St. Mark's Basilica under the direction of Giovanni Legrenzi. In 1699 Caldara became *maestro di cappella* (conductor) at the court of the Duke of Mantua. In 1701 he composed an opera that is now referred to by the phrase that is on the title page of the manuscript, *Opera pastorale*. It has the same anonymous libretto as *La costanza in amor vince l'inganno*, but none of the same music. The opening aria, *"Selve amiche,"* is in a major key.

Caldara moved to Rome to serve as the musical director of the household of Prince Ruspoli from 1709 to 1716. In 1710 Caldara wrote a new setting of this libretto for the public theater at Macerata. The opera was repeated in Rome the next year. At that time women were not allowed to perform on public stages in Rome, but because the performance took place in a private theater before an invited audience the role of Silvia was sung by a woman.

This is a *da capo* aria, but Caldara shortened the repetition of the first part by beginning it with the eighth measure.

Sources
(1) *La costanza in amor vince l'inganno*, manuscript score of the opera, Biblioteca musicale governativa del Conservatorio di Musica "S. Cecilia," Rome, G ms 184. In Act I, scene 1. For voice (soprano clef), two violins, viola and continuo. Original key: B minor.
(2) Same title, libretto for the 1711 performance, same library, Libretto XII.13.
(3) *Opera pastorale*, autograph score of the opera, Gesellschaft der Musikfreunde, Vienna, A 352.

This edition uses normal noteheads for the upper string parts and cue-sized notes for the editor's additions. The original has measures 1-4 played as a postlude; this edition shortens the postlude by using measures 17-18 instead.

"Smorzato" means dampened or softened, referring to the tone of the string orchestra.

Parisotti made a few changes in the bass line and added off-beat eighth notes in the accompaniment. Because long melismas were out of fashion in Parisotti's time, he provided an alternate version of the voice line with word repetitions to break up the melismas.

Luigi Dallapiccola also edited this aria (New York: International, 1961). He avoided certain Romanticisms of Parisotti's version but he did not work from the original score.

Selve amiche

Poet unknown

Antonio Caldara
Realization by John Glenn Paton

ⓐ Divide the note value equally between the two vowels.

Idiomatic translation: Friendly forest, shady trees, place where my heart finds shelter,

this loving soul asks you for some consolation in its sorrow.

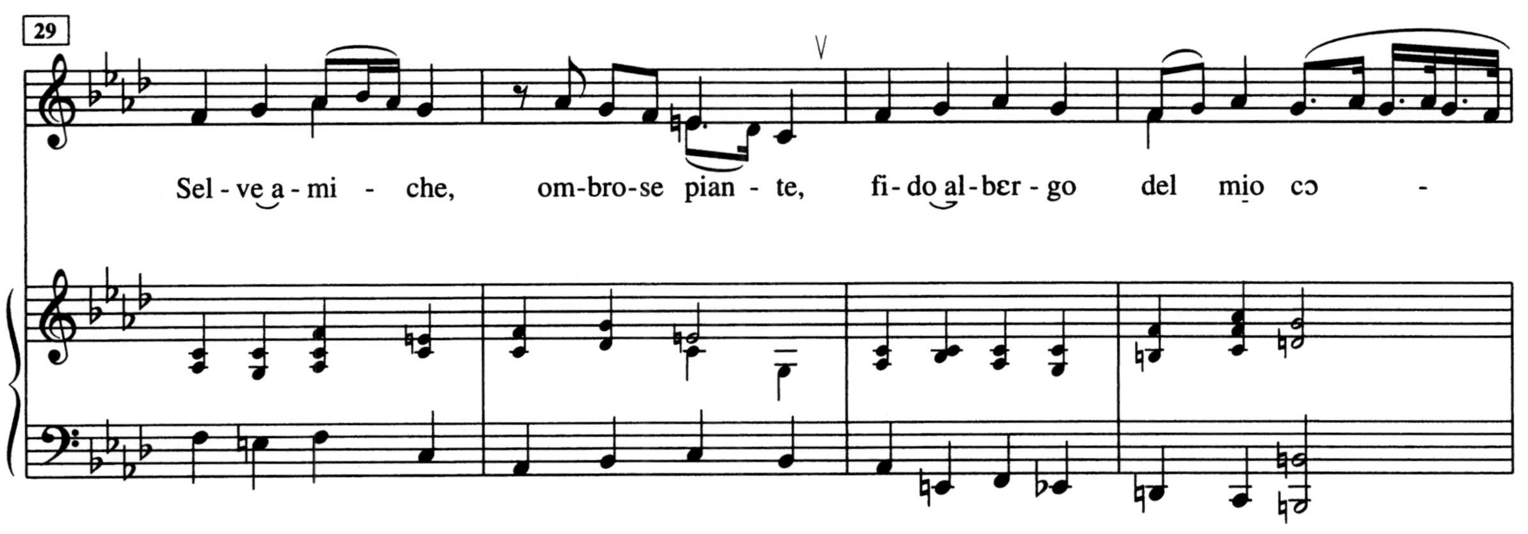
29
Sel - ve a - mi - che, om - bro - se pian - te, fi - do al - bɛr - go del mio cɔ -

33
- re, fi - do al - bɛr -

36
- go del mio cɔ - re!
tr

La rondinella amante

from *Griselda* (1735)
[grizɛlda]

Antonio Vivaldi
[antɔnjo vivaldi]
(Venice, 1678 – Vienna, 1741)

la rondinɛlːla amante
1 **La rondinella amante,**
The little-swallow loving,

lundʒi dal prɔprjo nido
2 **Lungi dal proprio nido,**
far from-the own nest,

sɛrba kostante fido
3 **Serba costante e fido**
keeps constant and faithful

al suo dilɛtːto il kɔr
4 **Al suo diletto il cor.**
to her delight the heart

non ɛ posːsibil mai
5 **Non è possibil mai**
Not is possible ever

katːʃar dal prɔprjo pɛtːto
6 **Cacciar dal proprio petto**
to-drive from-the own bosom

il radikato afːfɛtːto
7 **Il radicato affetto,**
the deep-rooted affection

il primo doltʃe amor
8 **Il primo dolce amor.**
the first sweet love.

Poetic idea
"A swallow, always faithful to its mate, can serve as a model to you and me." The singer is Corrado in the opera named after Queen Griselda of Sicily.

The fable-like story of Griselda comes from Boccaccio's *Decamerone*: the king sets out to test the faithfulness of his wife by subjecting her to cruel punishments. First he tells her that their daughter has been put to death by his command, then he banishes her from the court and announces that he will take a new wife.

In this aria Corrado is singing to Costanza, a young woman who is in love with Corrado's brother, Roberto. The king has chosen her against her will to be his new queen. Corrado is urging Costanza to remain faithful to Roberto. In fact, Corrado possesses secret information that Costanza is actually the daughter of the king and of Queen Griselda. He therefore knows that all will be well in the end, as it is when Griselda is restored to her throne and Costanza is allowed to marry Roberto.

According to the libretto, the male role of Corrado was sung by a woman in the first production.

Apostolo Zeno wrote the first libretto called *Griselda* in 1701, and at least fifteen composers set it to music. In 1735 a Venetian theater manager wanted to have the old libretto brought up to date. He hired a young writer, Carlo Goldoni, who later wrote the greatest comedies in the Italian language. The text of this aria was written by Goldoni, not by Zeno.

Background
Venice was home to Vivaldi, although he travelled extensively and composed music for many cities. He was a priest, but early in his career he ceased saying masses and devoted himself entirely to music. His chief employment was at the conservatory of the Ospedale della Pietà, an orphanage for girls. Vivaldi wrote concertos for the girls to play, and under his direction their orchestra was famous among music lovers. Of 45 or more operas he composed, 21 scores survive.

After a long period of neglect during which Vivaldi's music was virtually unknown even to professional musicians, he has emerged in recent years as a highly popular, much recorded composer.

Written late in Vivaldi's career, this da capo aria has a complex form that was used often in the late Baroque era. All of the musical ideas in the first part are presented twice: in measures 6-30, ending in the relative major key, then again in measures 31-52, ending in the tonic key (measures 53-67 are a codetta). Thus, the first part is itself in a binary form. The second part is still in a simple form, such as Alessandro Scarlatti used.

Sources
(1) *Griselda*, composer's autograph score of the opera, Biblioteca Nazionale, Turin, MS Foà 36. For voice (soprano clef), two violins, violas, and continuo. Original key: A minor.
(2) Libretto, Library of Congress, Washington, D. C., Schatz 10770.

This edition omits thirteen measures of instrumental music from the introduction and six measures of music from the interlude that begins in measure 69. Measures 57 and 61, which have parallel sixths between the two violins, have been simplified for the keyboard.

Both sources have been published in facsimile by Garland Publishing Co., New York, 1978, with a preface by Howard Mayer Brown.

This aria has never before appeared in an anthology.

La rondinella amante

Idiomatic translation: The loving swallow, far from her own nest, keeps her heart constant

and faithful to her beloved.

35
lun - gi dal prɔ - prio ni - do, sɛr - ba co -
39
stan - te, co - stan - te e fi - do, co - stan - -
44
- - - te e fi - do al suo
49
di - lɛt - - to il cɔr. La
f

53
ron - di - nɛl - la, la ron - di - nɛl - la a - man - te sɛr -
p
57
ba co - stan - te, sɛr - ba co -
60
stan - te il su - o di - lɛt - to co - stan - te il
f
63
cɔr, sɛr - ba co - stan - te, co - stan - te il cɔr.

It is not ever possible to drive from her heart that deep-rooted affection, her first sweet love.

S'en corre l'agnelletta

from *Ginevra, principessa di Scozia* (1720)
[dʒinɛvra printʃipɛs:sa di skɔtsja]

Domenico Sarro
[domeniko sar:ro]
(Trani, 1679 – Naples, 1744)

sen korːre laɲːɲelːletːta
1 S'en corre l'agnelletta
Along runs the-little-lamb

al tʃenːno del pastore
2 Al cenno del pastore
at-the signal of-the shepherd,

ne sa da lui partir
3 Né sa da lui partir.
nor knows-how from him to-part.

kwe lːlabːbro ke malːletːta
4 Quel labbro, che m'alletta
That lip that me-entices

dispor pwɔ del mio kɔre
5 Dispor può del mio core
dispose can over my heart

a vivere a morir
6 A vivere, a morir.
to live, to die.

Poetic idea

"Just as a little lamb follows a shepherd, I am dependent on my beloved for life or death." The singer is Dalinda, a noblewoman of the Scottish court, in an opera named after the king's daughter, Ginevra.

Dalinda loves a nobleman, Polinesso, and would do anything to please him. Polinesso wants to marry Ginevra and gain the throne of Scotland, but Ginevra is in love with Ariodante. In order to discourage Ariodante, Polinesso claims that he and Ginevra are already lovers. Polinesso persuades Dalinda to disguise herself as Ginevra and to admit him at night to a secret door of the castle. Ariodante witnesses this and believes that he has seen Ginevra letting Polinesso into her bedroom. Ariodante dashes off in despair to drown himself in the sea.

Dalinda regrets having played a role in the deceit. But Polinesso tells her that she is in danger and persuades her to run away. She exclaims that, having no will of her own, she will follow his will. She then sings this aria about her feelings of giving up control of her own life to her lover.

Polinesso treacherously sends two armed men to murder Dalinda, but she is rescued by Ariodante, who has miraculously avoided death. Dalinda confesses her role in deceiving Ariodante. At the end of the opera the truth is revealed and good triumphs. Dalinda, forgiven, marries Ariodante's brother.

The story of Ginevra comes from Ludovico Ariosto's epic poem *Orlando furioso*, cantos 4–6. At least a dozen operas were based on the story of Ginevra, sometimes under the title *Ariodante*.

Background

Sarro (also known as Sarri) studied in Naples and made his career there. Although not a major composer, he made innovations that prepared the way for the Classical style. Regular phrase-lengths in the melody and offbeat chords in the string accompaniment are two traits of this aria that became commonplace in the Classical era.

Sources

(1) Manuscript score of the opera, Bibliothèque Nationale, Paris, D. 14,296. This score is wrongly attributed to Leonardo Vinci on the title page. In Act II, scene 12. For voice (soprano clef), two violins, violas and continuo. Original key: F minor (signature of two flats).
(2) Manuscript score of the opera, Biblioteca del Conservatorio di Musica San Pietro a Majella, Naples, Rari 7.2.9. Attributed correctly to Sarro and dated 1720.
(3) *Arie 1721 in poi*, manuscript collection of arias, Biblioteca Casanatense, Rome, Ms. 2222, pp. 69-70. This is a short score, lacking the full string parts.

A libretto of *Ariodante* by Georg Wagenseil is reprinted in facsimile in *Italian Opera, 1640-1770*, vol. 93. *"S'en corre l'agnelletta"* is found in Act 2, scene 8.

Sarro used the six-measure introduction again after the first section and before and after the *da capo*. This edition shortens these sections to four measures.

Parisotti altered the playful rhythm of measure 8 by putting a slur over the first two notes. The original slur mark, connecting a weaker note to a stronger one, is characteristic of the Baroque era.

Sen corre l'agnelletta

Antonio Salvi

Domenico Sarro
Realization by John Glenn Paton

Andante, ♩ = 72–80

6

Sen cor - re l'a - gnel - let - ta_ al cen - no del pa - sto - re,_ al

11

cen - no del pa - sto - re né sa,___ né sa da lui par - tir,___ né

16

sa da_ lui par - tir, al cen - no del___ pa - sto - re né_

Idiomatic translation: The little lamb runs when the shepherd makes a gesture, and it never thinks of leaving him.

20
[or: lui par - tir.]
sa da_ lu - i par - tir.
Sen
26
cor - re l'a - gnel - let - ta_ al cen - no del pa - sto - re né sa,___ né sa,___ né
32
sa da lui par - tir,_____ né sa da_ lui par - tir, al cen - no del_ pa - sto - re né_
38
[or: lui par - tir.]
sa da_ lu - i par - tir.

Those lips that charm me are able to decide whether my heart will live or die.

63
Sen
a tempo
67
cor-re l'a-gnel-let-ta al cen-no del pa-sto-re, al cen-no del pa-
72
sto-re né sa, né sa da lui par-tir, né sa da lui par-
77
[or: lui par - tir.]
tir, al cen-no del pa - sto-re né sa da lu-i par-tir.

82
Sen cor - re l'a - gnel - let - ta_ al
88
cen - no del pa - sto - re né sa,___ né sa,___ né sa da lui par -
93
tir,___ né sa da_ lui par - tir, al cen - no del___ pa - sto - re né_
98
ritenuto
tr
sa da_ lu - i par - tir.
colla voce
a tempo
rit.

Consolati e spera

from *Ifigenia in Tauri* (1713)
[ifidʒɛnja in tauri]

Domenico Scarlatti
[domeniko skarlat:ti]
(Naples, 1685 – Madrid, 1757)

konsolati e spɛra
1 Consolati, e spera:
Console-yourself and hope;

potrai daltro od:ʒɛt:to
2 Potrai d'altro oggetto
you-will-be-able of-another object

pju ljɛto goder
3 Più lieto goder.
more happy to-enjoy.

la stel:la pju fjɛra
4 La stella più fiera,
The star most cruel,

se kandʒa daspɛt:to
5 Se cangia d'aspetto,
if it-changes in-aspect,

pwɔ aŋkoa laf:fan:no
6 Può ancora l'affanno
can yet the-worry

mutare in pjatʃer
7 Mutare in piacer.
change into pleasure.

Poetic idea
"Cheer up and hope; even the worst fate can change for the better." The singer is Dorifile, daughter of the king of Tauris. She is singing to Ismeno, who also has royal blood. She foresees a happy ending for herself, but he is pessimistic. (The librettist added these characters to form a romantic subplot to the original Greek tragedy.)

Background
Domenico Scarlatti, the sixth child of Alessandro and Antonia Scarlatti, was born in the same year as J. S. Bach and G. F. Handel. Trained by his father, Domenico became the organist of the royal chapel in Naples at the age of fifteen. In 1709 he moved to Rome, where he played the harpsichord in friendly competitions against Handel. In that year he also became the musical director at the court of the former Polish Queen Maria Casimira. Domenico composed seven operas for her private theater. All of them had librettos by her secretary, Capeci, and sets designed by the famous Filippo Juvarra. The sixth of these operas was *Ifigenia in Tauri*, created in 1713.

Later in life Scarlatti served the royal families of Portugal and Spain. Cut off from the opera world, he wrote hundreds of keyboard pieces, becoming one of the foremost keyboard composers of all time.

Sources
The complete score of *Ifigenia in Tauri* has been lost; two arias survive in:
(1) Manuscript collection of arias, Sächsische Landesbibliothek, Dresden, Mus. 1-F-30, pp. 96-98. For voice (alto clef), unison violins and continuo. Original key: A minor. Meter signature: C (but every measure contains two quarter-note beats).
(2) Libretto, Biblioteca musicale governativa del Conservatorio di Musica "S. Cecilia," Rome, G. Libretti Vol. 178.

The continuo part is silent during most of this aria. In the original score the unison violins either double the voice an octave above or move in imitation of it. Because the high register of the piano will not have the same brilliance as violins, this edition suggests playing the violin part in octaves.

Banck may have used the Dresden manuscript, but he gave the aria a highly romanticized treatment with a fully harmonized piano accompaniment throughout. Banck suggested a tempo marking of Andantino. In borrowing from Banck, Parisotti added a metronome marking of 44 to the quarter note, slowing the tempo to less than half the speed Scarlatti probably intended.

Consolati, e spera

Carlo Sigismondo Capeci

Domenico Scarlatti
Realization by John Glenn Paton

ⓐ If an introduction is desired, play measures 98–101.

Idiomatic translation: Cheer up and hope. You will yet have cause to be happy.

17
trai d'al - tro og - gɛt - to più liɛ - to go - der,
22
più liɛ - to go - der. Con -
27
so - la - ti: po - trai d'al - tro og - gɛt - to più
32
liɛ - to go - der, più liɛ - to go - der.

The most cruel fate can still change; anguish can yet be transformed into pleasure.

58
ta - re in pia - cer, mu - ta - re, mu - ta - re in pia -
tr
6
4
63
cer . Con - so - la-ti, e spε - ra: po -
f
tr
tr
p
70
trai d'al-tro og - gεt - to più liε - to go - der, più liε - to go -
75
der. Con - so - la - ti, e spε - ra: po -

80
trai d'al-tro og - gɛt - to più liɛ - to go - der,
85
più liɛ - to go - der. Con - so - la-ti:
91
po - trai d'al-tro og - gɛt - to più liɛ - to go -
96
der, più liɛ - to go - der.

Teco, sì

from *La caduta dei Decemviri* (1727)
[la kad<u>u</u>ta d<u>e</u>i detʃ<u>ɛ</u>mvi<u>r</u>i]

Leonardo Vinci
[leon<u>a</u>rdo v<u>i</u>ntʃi]
(Strongoli, ca. 1690 – Naples, 1730)

t<u>e</u>ko si v<u>ɛ</u>ŋgo aŋk<u>i</u>o
1 **Teco, sì, vengo anch'io**
You-with, yes, come also-I,

e m<u>e</u>ko vj<u>ɛ</u>ne am<u>o</u>r.
2 **E meco viene amor.**
and me-with comes love.

non pavent<u>a</u>r kɔr m<u>i</u>o
3 **Non paventar, cor mio,**
Not to-fear, heart my,

nɔ non pavent<u>a</u>r m<u>i</u>o kɔr
4 **Nò, non paventar, mio cor.**
no, not to-fear, my heart.

Poetic idea

"I am beside you as you go into danger. Have no fear." The singer is Icilio in the opera, *The Fall of the Decemvirate*, which is based on stories about the early days of Rome, as told by the historian Livy.

In 451 B.C.E. the Roman people elected a commission of ten men, the Decemvirate, to serve as administrators and judges. This experiment in government failed because one man, Claudius Appius, seized power and tried to rule as a tyrant.

In the opera Appius desires to possess a young woman named Virginia. He plots to gain power over her by having another man accuse her falsely of being his escaped slave. When Virginia is summoned to court, her fiancé, Icilio, reassures her in this aria that he will stand by her and protect her.

As Livy told the story, it ended tragically: Virginia's father murdered her rather than let her be dishonored by Appius. When Stampiglia wrote the libretto in 1697 for Alessandro Scarlatti, he gave it a happy ending. In both versions Appius's depravity was a principal reason why the Roman people overthrew the Decemvirate after they had ruled for only two years.

Background

As a youth, Vinci learned music at the conservatory of the Poveri di Gesu Cristo in Naples. Later in life he taught at the same school, and one of his students was Giovanni Battista Pergolesi.

Although Vinci's life was not long, he wrote more than twenty successful operas. This one, using a libretto that had already been set to music by several other composers, was first performed in Naples in 1727.

When Vinci's death was recorded, one church register said that he was 40 years old and another said that he was "about 34." It remains unclear just when he was born.

Source

La caduta dei Decemviri, manuscript score of the opera, Biblioteca dell'Abbazia, Montecassino, Ms. 126.E.23. In Act II, scene 10. For voice (soprano clef), violins, and continuo. Original key: C major. Meter: 3/8, but most measures contain six eighth notes. Original tempo: Allegro.

This edition shortens the introduction to the aria from 11 measures of 6/8 meter to 6 1/2 measures. The interlude before the return of the first section (measures 49-53) is just as Vinci wrote it.

Appoggiaturas in the voice part are notated just as in the original. They are doubled in the accompaniment, where all appoggiaturas are given in modern notation. In effect, the accompaniment shows the correct interpretation of the vocal ornaments.

Parisotti published this aria in the key of A-flat major. Parisotti adapted the aria to the taste of his time by breaking up the melismas with word repetitions.

Teco, sì

Silvio Stampiglia
Leonardo Vinci
Realization by John Glenn Paton
Allegro, ♩. = 50–56
5
Te - co,
3
3
8
sì, vɛn - go an - ch'i - o, e me - co vie - ne a - mor,
11
sì, me - co vie - ne a - mor, vie - ne a -

Idiomatic translation: I am also coming with you, yes, and with me comes love.

15
mor.
19
Te - co, sì, vεn - go an - ch'i - o, e me - co viε - ne a -
23
mor, [a - mor,] sì,
27
me - co viε - ne a - mor, viε - ne me - co, viε - ne a - mor,

Do not fear, my dear, no, do not fear.

49
53
Te - co, sì, vɛn - go an - ch'i - o, e me - co vie - ne a - mor,
57
sì, me - co viɛ - ne a - mor, viɛ - ne a - mor.
62
3
65
Te - co, sì, vɛn - go an - ch'i - o, e me - co viɛ - ne a -

ⓐ Cadenza suggested by the editor.

Stizzoso, mio stizzoso

from *La serva padrona* (1733)
[la sɛrva padrona]

Giovanni Battista Pergolesi
[dʒovanːni batːtista pergolezi]
(Iesi, 1710 – Pozzuoli, 1736)

stitːsozo mio stitːsozo
1 **Stizzoso, mio stizzoso,**
Peevish-one, my peevish-one,

voi fate il boriozo,
2 **Voi fate il borïoso,**
you play the conceited-one,

ma nɔ ma non vi pwɔ dʒovare
3 **Ma nò, ma non vi può giovare.**
but no, but not for-you can-it do-good.

bizɔɲːɲal mio divjɛto
4 **Bisogna al mio divieto**
It-is-necessary, at my prohibition,

star kwɛto e non parlare
5 **Star queto e non parlare.**
to-be silent and not to-talk.

tsit serpina vwɔl kozi
6 **Zit... Serpina vuol così.**
Hush, Serpina wills thus.

kredio ke mintendete si
7 **Cred'io che m'intendete, sì,**
Believe-I that me-you-understand, yes,

dakːke mi konoʃːʃete
8 **Dacché mi conoscete**
since me you-know

son molti e molti di
9 **Son molti e molti dì.**
are many and many days.

Poetic idea
"Don't think you can control me. I am in charge here." The singer is Serpina, a maid in the home of Uberto, a middle-aged bachelor. He is upset because she has been slow in bringing his morning cup of chocolate, but she is not going to let him dictate to her.

This scene is just the beginning of the comic events in which Serpina first dominates her employer and then makes him realize that he wants to marry her. Beginning as a *serva*, servant, she becomes the *padrona*, mistress of the house.

Background
In the 1600s many operas had comic servants whose antics provided relief from the serious problems of the more noble characters. Certain reformers in the early 1700s succeeded in banishing comic scenes from serious operas, and only a few comic operas were written.

In order to please members of the audience who enjoyed comedy, composers invented a new kind of comic opera, which was called *intermezzo* because it was performed during the intermission of a larger opera. Normally the two acts of the intermezzo were sandwiched between the three acts of a serious opera. Thus the audience heard two operas, often by two different composers, on the same evening. Intermezzi usually had only two or three characters, persons of low social station, and the plots were based on everyday life.

La serva padrona was first performed in 1733 in Naples between the acts of Pergolesi's *Il prigionier superbo*. One of the first intermezzi to be performed alone, separately from any serious opera, it spread quickly to all of the major opera centers. It was first published in Paris in 1752, where it caused a major controversy over the merits of Italian versus French music. *La serva padrona* had its first American performance in 1790 in Baltimore (in French), and it is still performed today by smaller opera companies.

Sources
No autograph score of *La serva padrona* exists. Three other early sources have been used for this edition.
(1) Untitled manuscript score of the opera, Conservatorio di musica, "G. Verdi," Milan, Ms. part. tr. 323a. Text of the title page: *"Dal Teatro Valle/ Intermezzo primo/ Uberto, Serpina, e Vespone servo che non parla/ Musica/ Del Sigr. Giambatta Pergolese/ 1735."* (Teatro Valle was in Rome.)
(2) *La serva padrona,* same library, Ms. part. tr. 323b.
(3) *La serva padrona*, Bischöfliche Zentralbibliothek, Regensburg, Germany, Pergolesi 2.1.

For voice (soprano clef), two violins, viola, and continuo. Original key: A major. No tempo marking. All three sources, which agree with each other except for minor errors, indicate the second violin and viola parts intermittently. The second violin usually doubles the first and the viola doubles the basses an octave higher. Only in a few measures do all of the strings have separate parts.

The dynamic and staccato markings in this edition all come from source (3); they are from the 1700s, but not original.

Parisotti used the more modern *"cheto"* [keto] for the older *"queto,"* which is in all three of the above sources. All three also attest the rhythm of measure 76, which Parisotti altered.

Stizzoso, mio stizzoso

Gennaro Antonio Federico

Giovanni Battista Pergolesi
Realization by John Glenn Paton

Idiomatic translation: My peevish one, you are acting conceited, but it will do you no good.
When I say no, you must be quiet.

Hush! That's how I want it.

46
f
p
ma non vi puɔ̀ gio - va - re. Bi - sɔ - gna al mio di - viɛ - to star quɛ -
f
dolce
52
to, quɛ - to e non par - la - re. Zit... zit...
p
59
f
Ser - pi - na vuɔl co - sì. Voi fa - te il bo - ri - o - so, ma non vi puɔ gio -
f
65
p
va - re. Bi - sɔ - gna al mio di - viɛ - to star quɛ - to e non par - la - re.
p

I think you understand me; you have known me for a long, long time.

ⓐ If an introduction is desired, begin here.

La Calandrina

from *L'Uccellatrice* (1751)
[lut:ʃel:latritʃe]

Niccolò Jommelli
[nik:kolɔ jom:mɛl:li]
(Aversa, 1714 – Naples, 1774)

ki vwɔl komprar la bɛl:la kalandrina
1 **Chi vuol comprar la bella calandrina**
Who wants to-buy the beautiful little-lark

ke kanta da mat:tina infino a sera
2 **Che canta da mattina infino a sera?**
that sings from morning until at evening?

ki vwɔl komprarla vɛŋga a kontrat:to
3 **Chi vuol comprarla, venga a contratto.**
Who wants to-buy-it, come to agreement

sɛmpre a bwɔn pat:to
4 **Sempre a buon patto**
Always at good terms

la venderɔ
5 **La venderò.**
it I-shall-sell.

Poetic idea
"Do you want to buy this little songbird? I'll give you a good price." The singer is Mergellina, and the opera is named after her profession: *"The Bird-Catcher."*

Both acts of this intermezzo take place in an open field where Mergellina catches birds to keep and sell. She encounters a hunter, Don Narciso, who falls in love with her immediately, mistaking her for a woodland goddess. She plays tricks on him, even snares him in a bird-net, but he is still infatuated with her.

Mergellina sings this aria at the opening of the second act. Of course, because this is a comic opera, she will meet Don Narciso again, and the story will have a happy ending after some complications.

Background
Jommelli studied in Naples, but his career took him to many cities. In 1751 he held a post at the papal chapel in Rome, but he wrote *L'Uccellatrice* for Venice. Later he directed the music at the ducal court in Stuttgart for 15 years, as his international fame increased.

Like *La serva padrona,* this *intermezzo* in two acts was originally performed as comic relief, sandwiched between the three acts of a serious opera.

Soon after its premiere *L'Uccellatrice* performed in Paris; it played a role in the lively dispute over the relative merits of French and Italian operas. Various productions of the intermezzo used various titles, such as *Il Paratajo* (The Net) and, in France, *La Pipée*, which means bird-catching by means of a trap or a call.

Source
No autograph score survives but this early source was used: Manuscript score, Conservatorio di musica, "G. Verdi," Milan, Noseda F 63. The title page says *"La Pipée, representé à Paris, sur le Théatre de l'Opéra."* For voice (soprano clef) and strings. Original key: D major.

In the score the introduction is 21 measures long, allowing time for the curtain to rise and for a bit of pantomime by the singer. This edition abbreviates the introduction.

A piano-vocal score of *L'Uccellatrice* was edited by Maffeo Zanon (Milan: Ricordi, 1954).

Gevaert published this aria with one stanza in Italian, two in French. Parisotti provided a second stanza in Italian; he may have written it himself, as it is in neither of the above scores.

La Calandrina

Poet unknown

Niccolò Jommelli
Realization by John Glenn Paton

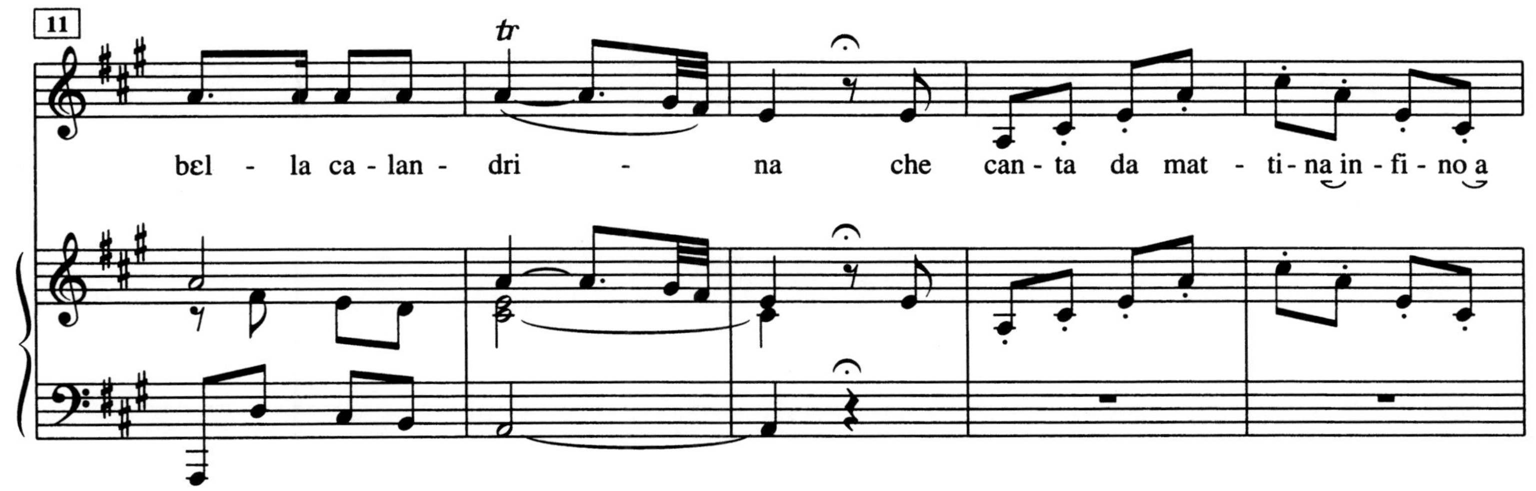

Idiomatic translation: Who wants to buy a pretty lark that sings from morning to

evening? Whoever wants to buy it, come to deal; I will sell it at a good price.

34
vuɔl, chi vuɔl com - prar - la? Chi? Chi? Vɛn - ga,
p
39
ⓐ ad lib.
vɛn - ga! [Ah!]
Sɛm-pre a buɔn pat - to la
f
p
42
vɛn - de - rò, sɛm-pre a buɔn pat - to la vɛn - de - rɔ̀.
tr
f
47

ⓐ Cadenza suggested by the editor.

Ogni amatore

from *La buona figliuola* (1760)
[la bwɔna fiʎːʎwɔla]

Niccolò Piccinni
[nikːkolɔ pitːʃinːni]
(Bari, 1728 – Passy, France, 1800)

ɛ meŋgɔtːto meŋgɔtːto
1 **Eh, Mengotto, Mengotto,**
Ah, Mengotto, Mengotto

di kwesto fjor si bɛlːlo
2 **Di questo fior si bello**
of this flower so beautiful

ke il tuo labːbro e il tuo kɔr vanta kozi
3 **Che il tuo labbro e il tuo cor vanta così**
that the your lip and the your heart boast so

intezi a dir kwesta kantsone un di
4 **Intesi a dir questa canzone un dì.**
I-meant to say this song one day.

oɲːɲi amatore
5 **Ogni amatore**
Every lover

nel prɔprjo kɔre
6 **Nel proprio core**
in his-own heart

il fjor damore
7 **Il fior d'amore**
the flower of-love

vantando va
8 **Vantando va.**
boasting goes.

ma dove naska
9 **Ma dove nasca**
But where is-born

la bɛlːla pjanta
10 **La bella pianta**
the beautiful plant

ke il labːbro vanta
11 **Che il labbro vanta**
that the lip boasts

nesːsuno il sa
12 **Nessuno il sa.**
no-one it knows.

Poetic idea
"My friend, you have been boasting about your faithfulness in love. But that reminds me of an old song that says 'Love is a beautiful flower, but no one knows where it grows.'" The singer is Cecchina in the opera *The Good Girl.* She is singing to a friend who has just boasted of his love for her.

One of the first English novels was Samuel Richardson's *Pamela, or Virtue Rewarded* (1740). Told in the form of letters, the novel recounted a young girl's successful resistance against her employer's attempts to seduce her. An immediate best-seller, the novel inspired both imitations and lampoons.

Translated into Italian by 1745, *Pamela* was turned into a play and later into an opera libretto by Carlo Goldoni, who also wrote the text of Vivaldi's *Griselda.* The libretto was first set to music by Egidio Duni in 1757, but Duni's music was forgotten after Piccinni composed his immensely popular version.

Background
The success of comic intermezzos such as *La serva padrona* and *L'Uccellatrice* encouraged composers to write full length comic operas that featured characters of humble birth involved in believable, every day problems. The new English sentimental novels and Rousseau's French writings in praise of naturalness made audiences want to see modern characters on stage.

La buona figliuola, although it was first performed in Rome by an all-male cast, became nevertheless an international success and a model for the new comic opera. Piccinni's music suited the characters: difficult arias for the affected persons of noble rank and simple, memorable tunes for the humbly born. Each act ended with a lengthy ensemble that consisted of multiple sections in various keys and moods; this innovation pointed the way toward Mozart's complex finales.

Source
No autograph score survives, but this early source was used: Manuscript score of the opera, Conservatorio di musica Luigi Cherubini, Florence. For voice (soprano clef) and strings. Original key: A major.

A photo-facsimile of the score and a libretto from Rome, 1760, are published in *Italian Opera 1640-1770*, preface by Eric Weimer (New York: Garland, 1983).

This edition includes the measures of recitative that directly precede the aria. The footnotes on the next page refer to two conventions of recitative notation. Appoggiaturas were not notated with printed signs in recitatives. The singer was expected to know that an appoggiatura can be sung whenever there are two identical notes, the first of which is accented. The appoggiatura is always a stressed syllable of text and usually a nonchord tone, adding color and expression to the recitative.

Much has been written about this opera. The literary aspect is analyzed wittily in "Pamela Transformed" by William C. Holmes, Musical Quarterly, 1952.

This aria has not been published in an anthology.

Ogni amatore

Carlo Goldoni

Niccolò Piccinni
Realization by John Glenn Paton

ⓐ Recitatives are normally written with long note values in the bass part, indicating how long the implied harmony remains unchanged. However, it is not necessary to sustain the chord for the full length of the written bass note. The chord may be re-played as often as one likes, or not re-played, provided that the singer feels comfortably supported by the sound.

ⓑ *A* indicates a note where the editor recommends an appoggiatura. Sing the next higher scale tone instead of the printed note. (The rule also permits appoggiaturas on the stressed syllables of *Mengotto* and *bello.*)

Idiomatic translation: Ah, Mengotto, regarding this flower so beautiful, about which your mouth and your heart are boasting, I have wanted to sing this song to you someday.

Every lover, in his own heart, is going to boast of the flower of love.

But where this lovely plant that is being talked about grows, no one knows.

49
la bel - la pian - ta che il lab - bro van - ta nes - su - no il
tr
54
sa. Ma do - ve na - sca,
p f
p
59
ma do - ve na - sca nes - su - no il sa, nes - su - no il
64
sa, nes - su - no il sa.
tr

Ombra cara amorosa

from *Antigona* (1772)
[antigona]

Tommaso Traetta
[tomːmazo traetːta]
(Bitonto, 1727 – Venice, 1779)

ombra kaɾa amoroza a perkemːmai
1 **Ombra cara amorosa, ah! perché mai**
Shade dear loving, ah, why ever

tu korːri al tuo ripɔzo ed io kwi rɛsto
2 **Tu corri al tuo riposo ed io qui resto?**
you run to your rest and I here remain?

tu traŋkwilːla godrai
3 **Tu tranquilla godrai**
You, peaceful, will-enjoy

nelːle sɛdi beate ove non dʒundʒe
4 **Nelle sedi beate ove non giunge**
in-the dwellings blessed where not arrives

ne zdeŋːŋo ne dolor dove rikɔpre
5 **Né sdegno né dolor, dove ricopre**
neither anger nor pain, where covers-again

oŋːŋi kuɾa mortale etɛrno obːblio
6 **Ogni cura mortale eterno obblio,**
Every care mortal eternal forgetfulness.

nepːpju ramːmenteɾai
7 **Né più rammenterai**
Nor more will-you-remember

fra ʎːʎamplɛsːsi patɛrni il pjanto mio
8 **Fra gl'amplessi paterni il pianto mio**
amid the-embraces paternal the weeping mine

ne kwesto di dolor sodːʒorno infɛsto
9 **Né questo di dolor soggiorno infesto!**
nor this of grief dwelling harmful.

io rɛsto sɛmpre a pjandʒeɾe
10 **Io resto sempre a piangere**
I stay always to weep

dove mi gwida oɲːɲor
11 **Dove mi guida ognor**
where me leads every-hour

duno in un altro orːror
12 **D'uno in un altro orror**
from-one into an other horror

la kruda sɔrte
13 **La cruda sorte.**
the cruel fate.

e a terminar le lagrime
14 **E a terminar le lagrime,**
And to end the tears,

pjetoza al mio dolor
15 **Pietosa al mio dolor,**
merciful to my sorrow,

ai ke non dʒundʒe aŋkor
16 **Ahi! che non giunge ancor**
alas! that not arrives yet

per me la mɔrte
17 **Per me la morte.**
for me the death.

Poetic idea

"Why have you died and left me alone and vulnerable? Why does not death come to take me, too?" The singer is Antigone, mourning for her brother, Polynice, who was slain in a duel with her other brother. The story comes from a Greek tragedy by Sophocles.

Background

Traetta studied in Naples under Durante. In this aria he used one of the most melancholy sounds of Neapolitan music, the lowered second scale degree (measures 5, 6 and 23).

Traetta's mature operas, written under the influence of Gluck, were intensely dramatic. His finest opera, *Antigona*, written in St. Petersburg, Russia, centers around this great aria of lamentation.

"Ombra cara amorosa" is an accompanied recitative, unusual in being in compound meter and in three-part form. Measures 8-11 and 16-20 need to be sung freely to produce a contrast between the recitative and the aria. The latter is in a rhythm known as *siciliana* or Sicilian rhythm.

Sources

Antigona, Act II, scene 1. Manuscript score of the opera, Staatsbibliothek Preußischer Kulturbesitz, Berlin, Mus. ms. 22008. For soprano, two violins, viola, and continuo. Original key: G minor.

An anonymous editor published this aria in *Collection de Chants Classiques* (copy in Civico Museo Bibliografico Musicale, Bologna, dated by hand 1850), including the cadenza that is shown here in measure 35. Banck elaborated the accompaniment so much that the recitative cannot be distinguished from the aria. Parisotti borrowed Banck's version, lowering it to E minor.

Selections from *Antigona* were published in score in *Denkmäler der Tonkunst in Bayern*, vol. 14:1 (Leipzig: Breitkopf und Härtel, 1914). Aldo Rocchi edited a full score (Florence: Maggio Musicale Fiorentino, 1962), based on two manuscript sources, one in Leningrad and the other in the Library of Congress, Washington, D. C.

Ombra cara amorosa

Marco Coltellini

Tommaso Traetta
Realization by John Glenn Paton

ⓐ Recitatives are normally written with long note values in the bass part, indicating how long the implied harmony remains unchanged. However, it is not necessary to sustain the chord for the full length of the written bass note. The chord may be re-played as often as one likes, or not re-played, provided that the singer feels comfortably supported by the sound.

Idiomatic translation: Dear loving spirit, why must you

ⓑ *A* indicates a note where the editor recommends an appoggiatura. Sing the next higher scale tone instead of the printed note.

go to your rest while I stay here? In peace you will enjoy the blessed dwellings where neither anger nor pain can enter,

where life's cares are hidden by eternal forgetfulness. In the embraces of your father you will no longer remember my weeping nor this terrible place.

© Cadenza suggested by an early editor, ca. 1850.

I stay here to weep always, led by a cruel fate from one horror

into another. And to end my tears, if only merciful death, alas!

would come for me!

ⓓ Cadenzas suggested by the editor.

Lungi da te, ben mio

(Undated; circa 1786-7)

Giuseppe Sarti
[dʒuzɛpːpe sarti]
(Faenza, 1729 – Berlin, 1802)

lundʒi da te bɛn mio
1 Lungi da te, ben mio,
Far from you, good mine,

si viver non pɔsːsio
2 Se viver non poss'io,
if to-live not can-I,

lundʒi da te ke sɛi
3 Lungi da te che sei
far from you that are

lutʃe deʎːʎɔkːki mjɛi
4 Luce degl'occhi miei,
light of-the-eyes mine,

vita di kwesto kɔr
5 Vita di questo cor,
life of this heart,

vɛŋga e in doltʃe sonːno
6 Venga e in dolce sonno,
come, and in sweet slumber,

se te miɾar non pɔnːno
7 Se te mirar non ponno,
if you to-admire not they-can,

mi kjuda i lumi aŋkor.
8 Mi chiuda i lumi ancor.
me close the eyes again.

Poetic idea

"If I may not live near you, please come and close my eyes lovingly as I die."

Background

Sarti worked as a conductor in Copenhagen for more than 20 years. Returning to Italy he produced a successful comic opera, *Le gelosie villane* (Country Jealousies), in Venice in 1776. After several more years in Copenhagen he became the music director of the cathedral in Milan; there he wrote an important serious opera, *Giulio Sabino*, performed in Venice, 1781, and also published in Vienna that year.

In 1784 Sarti was engaged to succeed Paisiello as court composer in St. Petersburg. As Sarti was traveling to Russia and Paisiello was returning to Italy, their paths crossed in Vienna. On June 9 Wolfgang Amadeus Mozart wrote to his father about his plans to attend a concert: "I shall take Paisiello along in the carriage to give him a chance to hear my compositions and my pupil's playing. If Maestro Sarti had not had to leave today, I would have taken him out there too. Sarti is a thoroughly honest, decent man! I played a great deal for him."

In the last scene of *Don Giovanni* Mozart quoted a melody from an opera by Sarti.

In 1785 Sarti hired a star singer to come to Russia: Luigi Marchesi, a soprano *castrato*. After great success in Russia, Marchesi left in 1787; Sarti stayed there for the rest of his career.

According to the research center, Ufficio Repertorio di Fondi Musicali, Milan, there are ten early manuscript sources of *"Lungi da te, ben mio"* in Italian libraries. All ten refer to *Le gelosie villane*, and one of them bears a notation "composed in Moscow." In fact, this aria is not found in any scores of the opera. Most probably Sarti composed it for Marchesi's use in performances of *Le gelosie villane* in Russia.

Marchesi also sang the aria for his London debut in 1788 in *Giulio Sabino*, using a similar text, *"Lungi dal caro bene."* Many published versions of the aria have used that text. (One newspaper reported that Marchesi had composed the aria himself, but no other evidence supports that idea.)

This music has thus been associated with two texts and with two operas, although it is not found in surviving scores of either one.

Sources

The four sources used for this edition all have the text *"Lungi da te, ben mio."* They differ from each other in minor details.

(1) Manuscript, Conservatorio di Musica Giuseppe Verdi, Milan, Noseda 2.12-2. For voice (soprano clef), two violins, two violas and continuo. Key: G major. Tempo: Andante.

(2) Manuscript, same library, Noseda 2.12-3. Same as (1) with addition of two horns in G. Tempo: Andante.

(3) Manuscript, same library, Noseda 2.12-4. Same as (2), but in A major. Tempo: Andante.

(4) Manuscript, Library of Congress, Washington, D.C, M1505. A1.196. For voice (soprano clef), two violins, two violas, and continuo. Key: G Major. Tempo: Andante grazioso. Preceded by an accompanied recitative 36 measures long; the text takes a female point of view.

(5) *Le gelosie villane*, libretto (Paris: L'Imprimerie de Monsieur, 1790), Act I, scene 6. Sung by a marquis to a country girl, Giannina.

Various printed editions were also consulted, none earlier than 1788.

Lungi da te, ben mio

Poet unknown

Giuseppe Sarti
Orchestral reduction by John Glenn Paton

ⓐ Play the ornament before the beat, as quickly as possible.

ⓑ *A* indicates a note where the editor recommends an appoggiatura. Sing the next higher scale tone instead of the printed note.

Idiomatic translation: Far from you, my beloved, if I am unable to go on living,

ⓒ Sing the appoggiatura as an eighth note and omit the note of resolution.

ⓓ Sing the ornamental note as the first of four equal notes.

far from you who are the light of my eyes and the life of my heart, come, and, if my eyes may not gaze on you, at least close them in a sweet sleep.

ⓔ Sing the ornamental note as the first of four equal notes.

ⓕ Sing the ornamental note as the first of four equal notes in spite of its appearance as an acciaccatura.

ⓖ Sing the first appoggiatura as an eighth note, and sing the second appoggiatura as the first of four equal notes.

Se voi bramate

from *Il re Teodoro in Venezia* (1784)
[il re teodoro in venεtsja]

Giovanni Paisiello
[dʒovanːni paizjεlːlo]
(Roccaforzata, 1740 – Naples, 1816)

skuzo lardire akmεt e atːʃεtːto il dono
1 Scuso l'ardire, Acmet, e accetto il dono.
I-excuse the-ardor, Akmet, and I-accept the gift.

bravo davːver da un turko tanto non atːtendea
2 Bravo davver! Da un Turco tanto non attendea.
Bravo really! From a Turk so-much not I-expected.

se segwirete apːprofitːtar kozi
3 Se seguirete a profittar così,
If you-continue to profit thus,

farete in brεve sotːto la skwɔla mia
4 Farete in breve, sotto la scuola mia,
you-will-do in short-time, under the school mine,

un onore imːmortale alːla turkia
5 Un onore immortale alla Turchia.
an honor immortal to Turkey.

se voi bramate
6 Se voi bramate
If you desire

il nɔstro amore
7 Il nostro amore
the our love,

larte imparate
8 L'arte imparate
the-art learn

di farvi amar
9 Di farvi amar.
of making-yourself to-be-loved.

ai sεnsi tεneri i doltʃi mɔdi
10 Ai sensi teneri i dolci modi,
To-the senses tender, the sweet ways,

a tratːto amabile sono kwei nɔdi
11 A tratto amabile sono quei nodi
to feature lovable are those knots

ke il kɔr vi pɔsːsono iŋkatenar
12 Che il cor vi possono incatenar.
that the heart for-you can enchain.

kol ruvido impεro
13 Col ruvido impero,
With rough authority,

kolːlaspra favεlːla
14 Coll'aspra favella,
with-harsh talking,

col tʃiʎːʎo severo,
15 Col ciglio severo,
with eye severe,

di dʒovane bεlːla
16 Di giovane bella
of young beauty

invan pretendete lafːfεtːto akːkwistar
17 Invan pretendete l'affetto acquistar.
in-vain you-expect the-affection to-acquire.

se aŋkor non lintεnde
18 Se ancor non l'intende,
If yet not it-he-understands,

tu mεʎːʎo sandrino
19 Tu meglio, Sandrino,
you better, Sandrino,

a kwel babːbuino
20 A quel babbuino
to that baboon

la skwɔla pwɔi far
21 La scuola puoi far.
the school you-can make.

Poetic idea

"I'll show you how to act around a lady. Roughness will get you nowhere." The singer is Belisa in *King Theodore in Venice.*

The opera is named after Baron Theodore de Neuhoff, a German who led an insurgency to free Corsica from its Genoese rulers. Crowned King of Corsica in 1736, he left the island two years later.

Belisa, King Theodore's sister, is a person of independent means. Also visiting Venice is Acmet, a deposed sultan of Constantinople. When Sandrino, a merchant, introduces Acmet to Belisa, she politely says, "Your humble servant." Acmet takes this literally and lays hands on her. She protests that her words were merely a polite phrase. Acmet offers her a large jewel; she only accepts it after he begs her to do so.

Belisa's words seem discriminatory against Turks, but in the 1800s Europeans still regarded Turkey as a hostile military power. Acmet is finally shown to be a generous person, when his great wealth rescues King Theodore from debtor's prison.

Background

Paisiello, a leading composer of comic operas, succeeded Traetta as the court composer in St. Petersburg. From Russia he went to Vienna, where he composed *Il re Teodoro in Venezia* and met Mozart.

Sources

1) Manuscript score of the opera, Harvard University. For voice (soprano clef), two oboes, two horns, and strings. Original key: F major.

(2) *Le roi Théodore à Venise* (Paris: Huguet, 1786), copy at University of California at Berkeley. As above, plus two flutes. Spoken dialogue and arias in French.

This aria is in no other anthology.

Se voi bramate

Giovanni Battista Casti

Giovanni Paisiello
Realization by John Glenn Paton

ⓐ Recitatives are normally written with long note values in the bass part, indicating how long the implied harmony remains unchanged. It is not necessary to sustain the chord for the full length of the written bass note. The chord may be re-played as often as one likes, or not re-played, if the singer feels comfortably supported by the sound.

ⓑ *A* indicates a note where it would be appropriate to sing an appoggiatura. Sing the next higher scale tone instead of the printed note.

Idiomatic translation: I excuse your ardor, Akmet, and accept your gift. Bravo! I did not expect it of you. If you continue to learn so quickly, under my tutelage you will soon turn out to be a great credit to your homeland.

If you desire our love, you must learn how to make us love you. To a person with tender sensibilities and a pretty face, sweet manners are the bonds that enchain the heart.

With rough commands, harsh speaking and stern eyes, you will try in vain to get the affection of a young beauty.

55
[de - te, in - van]
de - te, in - van pre - ten - de - te l'af - fɛt - to ac - qui - star.
60
Se voi bra - ma - te il nos - tro a - mo - re, l'ar - te im - pa -
65
ra - te di far - vi a - mar. L'ar - te im - pa - ra - te,
70
l'ar - te im - pa - ra - te... Se an - cor non l'in - tɛn - de, tu mɛ - glio, San - dri - no, a quel ba - bu -
Allegro, ♩. = 72–80
p
f
ⓒ

ⓒ Sing the grace note as an eighth note.

(If he still does not understand, Sandrino,

You will have to educate the ruffian.)

90
de - te l'af - fɛt - to ac - qui - star! In - van pre - ten - de - te l'af - fɛt - to ac - qui - star, l'af - fɛt - to ac - qui -
cresc.
94
star, l'af - fɛt - to ac - qui - star!
[Ah!]
Tempo primo
Se voi bra - ma - te
f
p
98
il nos - tro a - mo - re, l'ar - te im - pa - ra - te di far - vi a -
103
mar, l'ar - te im - pa - ra - te di far - vi a - mar,

ⓓ Cadenza suggested by the editor.

108
l'ar - te im - pa - ra - te di far - vi a - mar,
l'ar - te im - pa -
f
p
113
ra - te di far - vi a - mar,
l'ar - te im - pa - ra - te
f
p
118
di far - vi a - mar,
di far - vi a - mar,
di far - vi a -
f
p
f
p
123
mar, di far - vi a - mar.
f
p
f

Un bocconcin d'amante

from *"La Grotta di Trofonio"* (1785)
[la grɔtːta di trofɔnjo]

Antonio Salieri
[antɔnjo saljɛri]
(Legnano, 1750 – Vienna, 1825)

dika pur aristɔn tʃɔ keʎːʎiagːgrada
1 **Dica pur Ariston, ciò che gli aggrada;**
May-say indeed Ariston, that which him pleases;

la kɔza un brutːto aspɛtːto
2 **La cosa ha un brutto aspetto**
the thing has an ugly aspect,

e iŋkwjetetːsa mi da mi da sospɛtːto
3 **E inquietezza mi dà, mi dà sospetto.**
and disquiet me gives, me gives suspicion.

un bokːkontʃin damante
4 **Un bocconcin d'amante,**
A tasty-morsel of-lover,

trovato apːpena a un tratːto
5 **Trovato appena, a un tratto**
found hardly, at one stroke

skoprirlo pɔi per matːto
6 **Scoprirlo poi per matto,**
to-discover-him then for crazy

fapːprɔprjo male al kɔr
7 **Fa proprio male al cor.**
does really hurt to-the heart.

non vɔ kegːgrave savjo
8 **Non vò, che grave e savio**
Not I-want that, solemn and wise,

un amator manːnɔi
9 **Un amator m'annoi,**
a lover me-bores

magːgrave patːtso pɔi
10 **Ma grave e pazzo poi,**
but solemn and crazy, too,

kwesto ɛbːbɛn pɛdːʒo aŋkor
11 **Questo è ben peggio ancor.**
this is even worse yet.

fatʃɛto vivatʃe
12 **Faceto, vivace**
Jocular, lively,

vederlo mi pjatʃe
13 **Vederlo mi piace**
to-see-him me pleases,

ke skertsi ke rida
14 **Che scherzi, che rida,**
that he-jokes, that he-laughs

ke balːli ke kanti
15 **Che balli, che canti,**
that he-dances, that he-sings,

ke sɛmpre abːbja pronti
16 **Che sempre abbia pronti**
that always he-has ready

i fritːtsi rakːkonti
17 **I frizzi, i racconti,**
the quips, the tales,

i tratːti galanti
18 **I tratti galanti,**
the manners gallant,

le gaje parɔle
19 **Le gaie parole,**
the gay speeches,

il lɛpido umor
20 **Il lepido umor,**
the witty humor,

e se impatːtsar pɔi vwɔle,
21 **E se impazzar poi vuole,**
and if to-go-crazy then he-wants

impatːsi per amor
22 **Impazzi per amor.**
he-may-go-crazy for love.

Poetic idea
"Let me tell you what I want in a boyfriend!" The singer is Dori in the opera *The Grotto of Trofonio.*

Dori is one of the two daughters of Ariston. Dori is light-hearted, her sister is serious, and their respective lovers' temperaments match theirs perfectly. But when the men enter a cave owned by a magician, Trofonio, their personalities are mysteriously reversed.

In the aria Dori complains that her lover has become a thoughtful, solemn person, not at all her type. The opera ends happily when the magician changes the men back to their former selves.

Background
Salieri, a protegé of Gluck, rose to be music director of the imperial court in Vienna. He gave lessons to Beethoven and Liszt. Schubert prided himself on being a pupil of Salieri.

The Grotto of Trofonio was performed internationally for more than 20 years, with translations into English, Danish and German.

Salieri is unjustly remembered as a villain. In the 1820s there were rumors that he had murdered Mozart, but no serious historian believes them today.

Sources
La Grotta di Trofonio, full score of the opera (Vienna: Artaria, 1785; facsimile edition, Bologna: Forni, no date), Act II, scene 3. For voice (soprano clef), flute, two violins, viola and continuo. Original key: A major.

Un bocconcin d'amante

Giovanni Battista Casti

Antonio Salieri
Realization by John Glenn Paton

ⓐ Recitatives are normally written with long note values in the bass part, indicating how long the implied harmony remains unchanged. It is not necessary, however, to sustain the chord for the full length of the written bass note. The chord may be re-played as often as one likes, or not re-played, if the singer feels comfortably supported by the sound.

ⓑ *A* indicates a note where it would be appropriate to sing an appoggiatura. Sing the next higher scale tone instead of the printed note.

Idiomatic translation: Let him say whatever he likes, there's an ugly side to the matter. It causes me disquiet, even suspicion.

Having just found a delightful lover, suddenly to find out he's crazy, really makes you feel bad.

ⓒ Cadenza suggested by the editor.

I don't want a lover to bore me by being serious and wise, but to find out that he is serious and crazy is even worse.

ⓓ Play the ornaments on the beat, as the first of four 32nd notes.

I want to see my lover be clever, lively, joking and laughing, dancing and singing, always ready with quips and stories, with gallant manners, funny sayings, a witty way.

ⓔ Play these ornaments before the beat, as quickly as possible.

And if he wants to be crazy, let him be crazy about love.

79
que - sto è ben pεg - gio an - cor, è bεn pεg - gio an -
fp
cresc.
84
cor, è bεn pεg - gio an - cor.
Fa -
f
p
89
cε - to, fa - cε - to, vi - va - ce ve - der - lo mi pia - ce, che scher - zi, che ri - da, che
f
94
bal - li, che can - ti, che sεm - pre ab - bia pron - ti i friz - zi, i rac -
fp

99
con - ti, che sɛm-pre ab-bia pron - ti i friz-zi, i rac - con - ti, i trat - ti ga -
p
103
lan - ti, le ga - ie pa - rɔ - le, il lɛ - pi - do u - mor, e se im -paz-zar pɔi
107
vuɔ - le, im - paz - zi per a - mor, e se im - paz - zar pɔi
p
111
vuɔ - le, im - paz - zi per a - mor, im - paz-zi, im - paz-zi,
p

116
ma per a - mor, im - paz - zi, im - paz - zi
120
ma per a - mor, im - paz - zi per a -
123
mor, im - paz - zi per a - mor.
f
126

Antonia Bembo's autograph copy of *"In amor ci vuol ardir"* (pages 55–59) shown slightly reduced. This carefully written final copy was a gift to King Louis XIV. The top of the letter *A* was lost when the binder trimmed the pages. As in most cantata manuscripts, the voice is in soprano clef. The continuo part begins in the tenor clef (middle C on the fourth line) and changes to bass clef in measure 8. Notice that words are not placed under the notes in any precise way and that slurs are placed somewhat carelessly, never extending over more than three notes; this is also typical of cantata manuscripts from the period.

The Sounds of Italian

Italian is the favored language of great singers not only because of the beautiful music composed in that language, but also because the sounds of Italian are favorable to good singing. In learning to sing Italian correctly, one learns vocal habits that improve the singing of other languages as well.

These are some points of contrast between English and Italian:

- English emphasizes consonants, Italian emphasizes vowels. Strong emotions are conveyed in English by strong consonants, but in Italian by resonant vowels. Most English syllables end in consonants, but most Italian syllables end with vowel sounds.
- English speech is often broken by pauses, Italian almost never. English speakers often stop their tone in order to emphasize the coming word or to keep two vowels from running together, but Italians speak with continuous legato.
- English vowels may change color, Italian vowels are constant. The vowels in English "low" and "lay" are diphthongs, which change quality while they are being said; the similar Italian vowels in "lo" and "le" do not change quality no matter how long they last.
- English consonants sometimes change the color of nearby vowels, Italian ones do not. When an English vowel is followed by "l" or "r" (as in "steel" and "steer"), the consonant is likely to affect the vowel; in Italian this is not allowed to happen and the vowel remains pure.
- Some consonants are pronounced toward the back of the mouth in English, but toward the front of the mouth in Italian. In American speech, "r" involves the back of the tongue, but in Italian "r" is flipped or rolled with the tongue-tip.
- Italian consonants in general are weaker than English consonants. The sounds [p], [t] and [k] are sung without any escaping puff of air, and other consonant sounds are also weaker.

This last statement has a great exception: Italian double consonants are strong and clear. Compared with single consonants, double consonants take much more time to pronounce, even if they interrupt the musical line. For instance, in *petto* [pɛtːto], the symbol [ː] means "hold the consonant position." The first [t] stops the tone, and there is a brief silence before the second [t] begins it again.

Diphthongs

When two or more vowels are sung on a quick note, the note may be divided evenly among the vowels. When the note is longer, one vowel is selected to be the "syllabic vowel." It fills most of the note value, and the other vowels are pronounced quickly at the beginning or end of the note. This is especially important for the possessive pronouns *mio*, *tuo*, *suo*, and their various forms; in this book the syllabic vowels of these words are underlined for emphasis.

An Italian poet regards consecutive vowels an semi–vowels as forming one syllable, even if they belong to different words. For instance, in the phrase "*La cosa ha un...*," the sounds [a a u] belong to three different words and yet they are sung on only one note. In this book such combinations are indicated by a curved line connecting the words, and the syllabic vowel is underlined (see measure 3 of "Un bocconcin d'amante," page 148).

Key to the International Phonetic Alphabet for Italian

Vowels

A	[a],	bright, smiling "ah," as in	*cara* [kara], *andante* [andante]
E	[e],	"closed," as in	*che* [ke], *legato* [legato]
	[ɛ],	"open," as in	*ecco* [ɛk:ko], *presto* [prɛsto]
I	[i],	as in	*mio* [mio], *divino* [divino]
O	[o],	"closed," as in	*solo* [solo], *così* [kosi]
	[ɔ],	"open," as in	*opera* [ɔpera], *forte* [fɔrte]
U	[u],	as in	*bruno* [bruno], *tuba* [tuba]

(Italian spelling does not show when e and o are pronounced closed and when they are open. For your convenience this book shows the open e's and o's with IPA symbols inserted into the Italian words.)

Semi-Vowels

I	[j],	before another vowel, as in	*più* [pju], *piano* [pjano]
U	[w],	before another vowel, as in	*uomo* [wɔmo], *acqua* [ak:kwa]

Consonants

B, F, M, and V are pronounced as in English.

D, N, T, and L are pronounced as in English, but with the tongue contacting the upper teeth.

C	[tʃ],	before e or i, as in	*cielo* [tʃɛlo], *cello* [tʃɛl:lo]
C	[k],	otherwise, as in	*orchestra* [orkɛstra], *cantata* [kantata]
SC	[ʃ],	before e or i, as in	*scena* [ʃɛna], *crescendo* [kreʃɛndo]
SC	[sk],	as in	*scala* [skala], *scherzo* [skɛrtso]
G	[dʒ],	before e or i, as in	*gentile* [dʒentile], *regina* [redʒina]
G	[g],	otherwise, as in	*grande* [grande], *largo* [largo]
N	[ŋ],	before [k] or [g], as in	*ancora* [aŋkora], *languire* [laŋgwire]
QU	[kw],	as in	*quasi* [kwazi], *quartetto* [kwartet:to]
R	[ɾ],	flipped between two vowels, as in	*furore* [fuɾoɾe], *cara* [kaɾa]
R	[r],	trilled in all other cases, as in	*ritardo* [ritardo], *cor* [kɔr]
S	[s],	as in	*secco* [sɛk:ko], *sostenuto* [sostenuto]
S	[z],	in some words, as in	*deciso* [detʃizo], *slancio* [zlantʃo]
Z	[ts],	as in	*terzetto* [tertset:to], *grazia* [grat:tsja]
Z	[dz],	in some words, as in	*mezzo* [mɛd:dzo]

Gliding Consonants (not found in English)

GLI	[ʎ],	like [lj] but made with the middle of the tongue, as in	*scoglio* [skɔʎ:ʎo], *taglia* [taʎ:ʎa]
GN	[ɲ],	like [nj] but made with the middle of the tongue, as in	*ogni* [oɲ:ɲi], *segno* [seɲ:ɲo]

Silent Letters

H is always silent, as in	*hanno* [an:no], *honestà* [onesta]
H hardens C, G, and SC, as in	*chi* [ki], *meschino* [meskino]
I is silent when used to soften C, G, or SC, as in	*già* [dʒa], *lascia* [laʃ:ʃa]

Please note: Phonetic symbols show the similarities that exist between the sounds of different languages. Nevertheless, they have slightly different values in different languages, and phonetic transcriptions can only be approximate. One still needs to listen to the way the language is sung by native Italians. Furthermore, many singers employ vowel modification, and phonetic transcriptions do not show this. The vowel pronunciations given in this book come from Zingarelli's *Vocabolario della lingua italiana*; they may be modified to accommodate your voice.

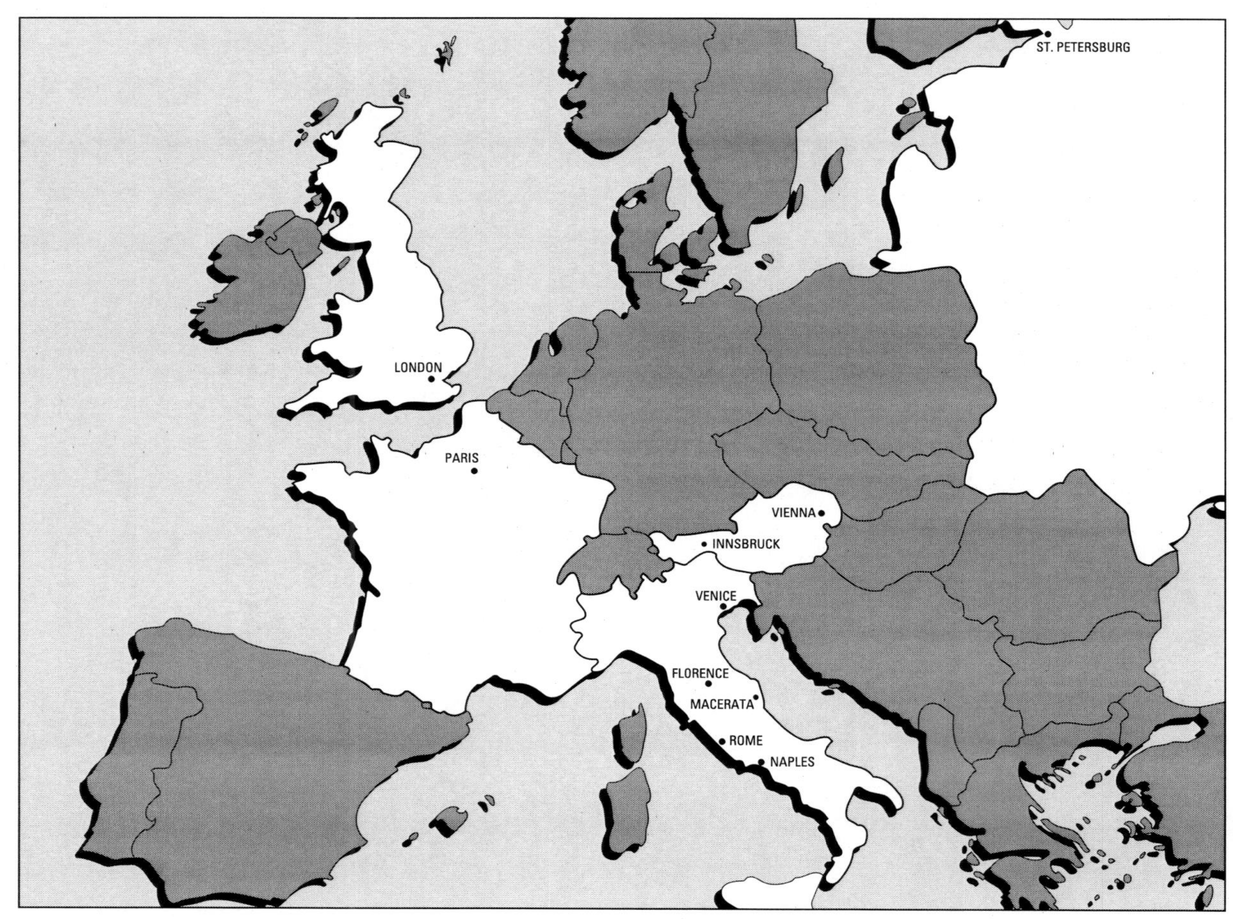

Geographical Origins

1. PERI..................................Nel pur ardor ....Florence
2. FALCONIERI......................Vezzosette e care pupillette ....Rome?
3. F. CACCINI ....Che t'ho fatt'io..Florence
4. CARISSIMI ....Piangete, ohimè piangete ....Rome
5. LORI..................................Dimmi, amor..Rome
6. CAPROLI ....Tu mancavi a tormentarmi.......................................Rome
7. CESTI ....Si mantiene il mio amor ....Venice
8. CESTI ....Intorno all'idol mio ....Innsbruck
9. BEMBO ....In amor ci vuol ardir ....Paris
10. A. SCARLATTI ....Toglietemi la vita..Rome
11. A. SCARLATTI..................Amor, preparami ....Rome
12. BONONCINI ....Deh, più a me non v'ascondete ....Rome
13. BONONCINI ....L'esperto nocchiero ....Rome
14. BONONCINI ....Un'ombra di pace ....London
15. CALDARA ....Selve amiche...Macerata/Rome
16. VIVALDI ....La rondinella amante ....Venice
17. SARRI................................Sen corre l'agnelletta...Naples
18. D. SCARLATTI ....Consolati, e spera...Rome
19. VINCI ....Teco, sì...Naples
20. PERGOLESI ....Stizzoso, mio stizzoso ....Naples
21. JOMMELLI ....La Calandrina...Venice
22. PICCINNI ....Ogni amatore...Rome
23. TRAETTA...........................Ombra cara, amorosa ....St. Petersburg
24. SARTI ....Lungi da te, ben mio ....St. Petersburg?
25. PAISIELLO ....Se voi bramate ....Vienna
26. SALIERI ....Un bocconcin d'amante...Vienna